HYMNS

90 DEVOTIONS FROM

OUR DAILY BREAD

COMPILED BY DAVE BRANON

1-19-16

Discovery House.
from Our Daily Bread Ministries

Previously published as *Tune My Heart to Sing: 90 Devotions on Hymns from Our Daily Bread*.

Discovery House is affiliated with Our Daily Bread Ministries, Grand Rapids, Michigan.

Requests for permission to quote from this book should be directed to: Permissions Department, Discovery House, P.O. Box 3566, Grand Rapids, MI 49501, or contact us by e-mail at permissionsdept@dhp.org.

ISBN: 978-1-62707-489-6

Printed in the United States of America
First printing in 2016

CONTENTS

FOREWORD

Years ago, while turning the dial of a shortwave radio one night in Kenya, I came across the voice of a man speaking rapidly in German until he pronounced the next singer's name: "Willie Nelson." I laughed aloud at the incongruity of being in East Africa and listening to a German disc jockey introduce an American country singer. How old-fashioned that seems in today's digital age. Yet, from the concert halls of great cities to the campfires of remote villages, "the universal language" of music still touches the hearts and souls of people across the globe.

How true this is among the followers of Jesus Christ. The story of God's work on earth began with music during creation when "the morning stars sang together and all the angels shouted for joy" (Job 38:7). It continued with David's songs of adoration, confession, and thanksgiving, followed by Jeremiah's mournful lament over the spiritual failure of God's people. It will conclude when we sing His praise forever in heaven (Revelation 19:5). As we await that day, we are encouraged to "be filled with the Spirit, speaking to one another with psalms, hymns, and songs from the Spirit. Sing and make music from your heart to the Lord" (Ephesians 5:18–19).

The songs of faith that mean most to us capture our deepest emotions and wrap them in words and melodies we remember. They guard us on the heights of success and guide us through the valleys of despair.

In 1757, twenty-two-year-old Robert Robinson penned these words:

> *Come, Thou Fount of every blessing,*
> *tune my heart to sing Thy grace;*
> *Streams of mercy, never ceasing,*
> *call for songs of loudest praise.*

Teach me some melodious sonnet
sung by flaming tongues above;
Praise the mount—I'm fixed upon it—
mount of Thy redeeming love.

Hymns celebrates the power of songs and hymns in our lives. What a privilege it is to pour out our pleas for help and our praise to our God of grace, whose love never fails!

—*David McCasland*

THANK GOD FOR MUSIC

Read: 2 Chronicles 5:7-14

The trumpeters and singers joined in unison . . . . The glory of the LORD filled the temple of God. —2 CHRONICLES 5:13–14

Music plays a big part in the Bible. From Genesis to Revelation, God enlists musicians to work on His behalf. He uses music to call people to worship and to send them to war, to soothe ragged emotions and to ignite spiritual passion, to celebrate victories and to mourn losses. Music is an all-occasion, all-inclusive art form. There are followers and leaders, simple songs and complex songs, easy instruments and difficult instruments, melodies and harmonies, fast rhythms and slow rhythms, high notes and low notes.

Music is a wonderful metaphor for the church because everyone participates by doing what he or she does best. We all sing or play different notes at different times, but we all perform the same song. The better we know our parts, and the better we follow the conductor, the more beautiful the music.

One of the best uses for music is praise. When Solomon's temple was completed, the musicians praised and thanked God. As they did, "the glory of the LORD filled the temple of God" (2 Chronicles 5:14).

We thank God for beautiful music, for it's like a preview of heaven, where the glory of God will dwell forever and where praise for Him will never cease.

—*Julie Ackerman Link*

———

While musical styles can be controversial, we can also celebrate the fact that God can be glorified with the variety of music He has allowed to be developed. While some may prefer Fanny Crosby over Chris Tomlin (or vice versa), the beauty of unity in Christ is that we can overlook differences to stand together in praise of our heavenly Father in song.

ROCKS AND DIAMONDS

Read: Psalm 18:30-36

The LORD is my rock, my fortress and my deliverer; my God is my rock, in whom I take refuge. —PSALM 18:2

The story is told of a preacher named Augustus Toplady, who was taking a walk through the English countryside when a sudden storm swept across the landscape. Toplady spotted a wide rock formation with an opening—a cleft—where he sought shelter until the storm passed. As he sat out the deluge, he contemplated the connection between his shelter and God's help in life's storms.

He had no paper on which to write, but he found a playing card on the floor of the cavelike structure and began to write the words to the beloved hymn "Rock of Ages."

Written on that stormy day in 1775, this hymn has been a source of strength for Christians ever since.

> *Rock of ages, cleft for me,*
> *Let me hide myself in Thee;*
> *Let the water and the blood,*
> *From Thy wounded side which flowed,*
> *Be of sin the double cure,*
> *Save from wrath and make me pure.*

Think of your struggles. Do you need a place to hide? Do you need someone to shelter you from life's assaults? Do you need the assurance that you've been forgiven? As Toplady experienced, we can find shelter and assurance in God.

Don't stand out in life's storms alone. Seek God's shelter. Ask Him to protect you. Make sure you have received His forgiveness. Get close to the Rock of Ages. It's life's safest spot.

—*Dave Branon*

The hymn "Rock of Ages" first appeared in the *Gospel Magazine* in 1775, which Augustus Toplady edited for two years. The magazine is still in publication.

COME HOME

Read: Psalm 51:1-13

Restore to me the joy of your salvation and grant me a willing spirit, to sustain me. —PSALM 51:12

As 19-year-old Amelia sat in the waiting room of her doctor's office, she recognized the familiar hymn "Softly and Tenderly Jesus Is Calling" playing over the speaker. It made her smile when she remembered the words. Perhaps a song with the lyrics "shadows are gathering, deathbeds are coming" was not the most appropriate background music for folks waiting to see the doctor!

Some find this old hymn too sentimental for their taste. But the message of the chorus can be encouraging for the wayward sinner:

> *Come home, come home;*
> *Ye who are weary, come home;*
> *Earnestly, tenderly, Jesus is calling—*
> *Calling, "O sinner, come home!"*

When a believer replaces God's will with his own, he will find himself in a backslidden condition, out of fellowship with God, and in an unenviable state. Although we sometimes yield to our self-centered nature, God is always ready to welcome us back. Because of His "unfailing love" and "great compassion," it gives Him joy when we forsake our rebellious ways, return to Him, and ask for forgiveness (Psalm 51:1–2; Luke 15).

Has your heart and mind slipped away from your Savior? Jesus is calling and waiting for you to come back home.

—*Cindy Hess Kasper*

"Softly and Tenderly Jesus Is Calling," which was written by Will L. Thompson in 1880, was sung at a memorial service for Martin Luther King Jr. at Ebenezer Baptist Church on April 8, 1968.

BY GOD'S HELP

Read: 1 Samuel 7:2-12

Then Samuel took a stone and set it up between Mizpah and Shen. He named it Ebenezer, saying, "Thus far the LORD has helped us."
—1 SAMUEL 7:12

The word *Ebenezer* in the hymn "Come, Thou Fount of Every Blessing" reminds us of a time when the people of Israel were trying to regain the close relationship they once had with God. Their spiritual leader, Samuel, told them that if they would abandon their foreign gods and return to the Lord wholeheartedly, He would deliver them from being oppressed by their enemy, the Philistines (1 Samuel 7:2–3).

When the people turned from their sin, God gave them victory. In response, "Samuel took a stone and set it up between Mizpah and Shen. He named it Ebenezer, saying, 'Thus far the LORD has helped us' " (v. 12).

When we sing,

> *Here I raise my Ebenezer—*
> *Hither by Thy help I've come;*
> *And I hope, by Thy good pleasure*
> *Safely to arrive at home*

we are reminded that in our times of need we can always turn to God to find forgiveness and help. Whatever we have done, wherever we have wandered, He will receive and restore us by His grace.

A small stone on a desk or shelf can be our own Ebenezer— a powerful, visible reminder that by God's help we have come this far in life, and He will see us through to the end.

—*David McCasland*

"Come, Thou Fount," which begins "Come, Thou Fount of every blessing, tune my heart to sing Thy grace," was written in the eighteenth century in England by Robert Robinson, but it is still popular today. It has been recorded by groups such as the David Crowder Band and Jars of Clay.

𝄇

THE GOOD STORY

Read: Luke 23:44-24:3

*They found the stone rolled away from the tomb, but when they entered,
they did not find the body of the Lord Jesus.* —LUKE 24:2–3

People tend to remember negative images more than they do positive ones, according to an experiment conducted at the University of Chicago. While people claim that they want to turn away from the barrage of bad news in the media, this study suggests that their minds are drawn to the stories.

Katherine Hankey (1834–1911) was more interested in the "good news." She had a desire to see young women come to know Christ. In 1866, she became very ill. As she lay in bed, she thought about those with whom she had shared the story of Jesus' redemption, and she wished that someone would visit and comfort her with "the old, old story." That's when she wrote a poem that later became the hymn "Tell Me the Old, Old Story."

> *Tell me the story slowly, that I may take it in—*
> *That wonderful redemption, God's remedy for sin.*
> *Tell me the story often, for I forget so soon;*
> *The early dew of morning has passed away at noon.*

We never tire of hearing the story that because of His great love God sent His one and only Son to this earth (John 3:16). Jesus lived a perfect life, took our sin upon himself when He was crucified, and three days later rose again (Luke 23:44–24:3). When we receive Him as our Savior, we are given eternal life and become His children (John 1:12).

Tell someone the old, old story of Jesus and His love. That person just might need some good news.

—Anne Cetas

According to Ira Sankey, Katherine Hankey's poem was read at a YMCA convention in 1867. William Howard Doane heard the poem and later wrote the music for it.

IS IT WELL?

Read: Philippians 4:4-7

The peace of God, which transcends all understanding, will guard your hearts and your minds in Christ Jesus. —PHILIPPIANS 4:7

As the high school chorale prepared to sing Horatio G. Spafford's classic hymn, "It Is Well with My Soul," a teen stepped forward to tell the song's familiar history. Spafford wrote the song while on a ship that was near the spot at sea where his four daughters perished in a collision of two ocean-going vessels.

As I listened to that introduction and then the words sung by the teenagers, a flood of emotions washed over me. "Where his four daughters perished" were hard words to grasp as I listened again to Spafford's words of faith. Having lost one teenage daughter suddenly myself, I find the idea of losing four unfathomable.

How could it be "well" for Spafford in his grief? I hear the words "When peace, like a river, attendeth my way" and remember where peace can be found. Paul says in Philippians 4 that it can be found as our heart-prayers are voiced to God (v. 6). By trustful praying, we unburden our hearts, divest our anxieties, and release the grip on our grief. And we can gain "the peace of God" (v. 7)—an inexplicable, divine calmness of spirit. This peace supersedes our ability to understand our circumstances (v. 7), and it is a guard on our heart, through Jesus, that protects us enough to allow us to whisper, even in the pain, "It is well with my soul."

—*Dave Branon*

Horatio and Anna Spafford lost their only son to pneumonia in 1870 before losing their daughters (Annie, 11; Margaret, 9; Bessie, 5; and Tanetta, 2) in the November 22, 1873, shipwreck of the *Ville du Havre* while Anna and the girls were on their way to a vacation in England.

THE FAIREST

Read: Revelation 5:8-14

Worthy is the Lamb, who was slain. —REVELATION 5:12

When I first became a Christian and started attending church at age nineteen, I immediately fell in love with the great hymns of the faith. My heart overflowed with joy and thanksgiving as we sang of God's love for us in Christ. Soon one of my favorite hymns (written in the late 1600s) became "Fairest Lord Jesus." I love the simplicity of the melody and the awesomeness of the One exalted in these words:

> *Fair is the sunshine, Fairer still the moonlight,*
> *And all the twinkling starry host: Jesus shines brighter,*
> *Jesus shines purer than all the angels heaven can boast.*
> *Beautiful Savior! Lord of the nations!*
> *Son of God and Son of Man!*
> *Glory and honor, praise, adoration*
> *Now and forevermore be Thine!*

God's Son, whom we sing about in this song, came to this earth, lived a perfect life, and gave himself for us on the cross (Luke 23:33). He arose from the grave (Luke 24:6) and is now seated at God's right hand (Hebrews 1:3). One day we'll join in worship with thousands upon thousands and say: "To him who sits on the throne and to the Lamb be praise and honor and glory and power, for ever and ever!" (Revelation 5:13). Maybe we'll sing "Fairest Lord Jesus" too.

Until then, let's allow Jesus to be "the fairest" above all in our personal lives by seeking wisdom from His Word and following in His ways.

—*Anne Cetas*

Not much is known about the history of "Fairest Lord Jesus." It appears to have been published in English for the first time in 1677.

HE WATCHES ME

Read: Matthew 10:16-31

So don't be afraid; you are worth more than many sparrows.
—MATTHEW 10:31

One Sunday morning at church, we sang "His Eye Is on the Sparrow" as a congregational hymn. It was a rare opportunity to give voice to a song usually performed by a soloist.

During the first chorus, I noticed a friend who was weeping so hard he couldn't sing. Knowing a bit of what he had been through recently, I recognized his tears as ones of joy at realizing that, no matter what our situation, God sees, knows, and cares for us.

Jesus said, "Are not two sparrows sold for a penny? Yet not one of them will fall to the ground outside your Father's care. And even the very hairs of your head are all numbered. So don't be afraid; you are worth more than many sparrows" (Matthew 10:29–31). The Lord spoke these words to His twelve disciples as He sent them out to teach, heal, and bear witness of Him to "the lost sheep of Israel" (v. 6). He told them that even though they would face persecution for His sake, they should not be afraid, even of death (vv. 22–26).

When threatening circumstances press us to lose hope, we can find encouragement in the words of this song: "I sing because I'm happy, I sing because I'm free. For His eye is on the sparrow, and I know He watches me." We are under His watchful care.

—David McCasland

The writer of the words to "His Eye Is on the Sparrow," Civilla Martin, said she heard a disabled friend answer a question about the secret to her happiness despite her troubles by saying, "His eye is on the sparrow, and I know He's watching me." Singer Ethel Waters used the song title as the title of her autobiography.

SOMETHING TO SING ABOUT

Read: Psalm 147

Praise the LORD. How good it is to sing praises to our God.
—PSALM 147:1

I understand why I was never asked to join a choir or sing a solo. Musical talent was never one of my gifts. I discovered this at nine years of age when I was outside on our farm one day singing lustily. My mother opened the door and asked, "Is one of the calves sick? I think I just heard one."

My mother's words have never kept me from praising God in song, however. And when I preached somewhere, I enthusiastically joined in congregational singing (making sure, of course, not to stand too close to the microphone).

God's great salvation fills me with gratitude, and one way to express my joy is to sing about it. That's why I'm puzzled by people who say they are Christians but admit that they seldom attend church services, almost never listen to Christian music, and find singing hymns and listening to sermons boring. I can understand nonbelievers saying this because they know neither God nor the joy of salvation. But believers do!

Reflect often and deeply on the riches you have in Christ. If you feel joyful, you will want to praise the Lord. And even if you are a poor singer like me, you'll still say a hearty "Amen" to the psalmist's words: "How good it is to sing praises to our God" (Psalm 147:1).

—*Herb Vander Lugt*

According to one survey conducted by the Barna Group, fifteen percent of people in the United States who identified themselves as Christians do not go to church.

THE VALUE OF "HUMS"

Read: Psalm 126:1-3

Speaking to one another with psalms, hymns, and songs from the Spirit.
—EPHESIANS 5:19

Do you know why bees hum? It's because they can't remember the words!

Ironically, that old joke reminds me of a serious story I read about a man awaiting heart bypass surgery. He was aware that people die during surgery. As he thought about all that could go wrong, he felt very much alone.

Then an orderly walked into his room to take him to surgery. As the young man began to push the patient's gurney along the corridor, the patient heard the orderly humming the ancient Irish hymn "Be Thou My Vision." It prompted his memories of lush green fields and the ancient stone ruins of Ireland, the land of his birth. The hymn flooded his soul like a fresh breath of home. When the orderly finished with that song, he hummed Horatio Spafford's hymn, "It Is Well with My Soul."

When they stopped outside the surgical suite, the patient thanked the orderly for the hymns. "God has used you this day," he said, "to remove my fears and restore my soul." "How so?" the orderly asked in surprise. "Your 'hums' brought God to me," the man replied.

"The LORD has done great things for us" (Psalm 126:3). He has filled our heart with song. He may even use our "hums" to restore someone's soul.

—David Roper

"Be Thou My Vision" originated more than 1,000 years ago in Ireland. It was translated into English by Mary Byrne and popularized in the early twentieth century.

INVISIBLE MAN

Read: John 14:5-20

Fixing our eyes on Jesus, the pioneer and perfecter of faith. For the joy set before him he endured the cross. —HEBREWS 12:2

As a boy, I was fascinated by the book *The Invisible Man.* The main character played an elaborate game of hide-and-seek, staying just out of reach of mere mortals "cursed" with a visible nature. To have a physical presence, he wore clothes and wrapped his face in bandages. When it was time to escape, he simply removed everything and disappeared.

I wonder if we have similar thoughts about our unseen God. We feel He's beyond our reach, as expressed in a stanza of one of my favorite hymns: "Immortal, invisible, God only wise, in light inaccessible hid from our eyes."

Yet, while declaring the wonder of God, the hymn speaks of a God who is not just invisible: "All praise we would render—O help us to see 'tis only the splendor of light hideth Thee!"

We perceive that God is distant, far off, inaccessible, and hidden. But we need a God who is accessible, and we wonder how to have a meaningful relationship with Him. We will never fully comprehend what God is like. Yet He himself is accessible to us. In part, that is why Jesus came—to "show us the Father" (John 14:8) and to bring us close to Him, because "the Son is the image of the invisible God, the firstborn over all creation" (Colossians 1:15).

Our God is invisible—beyond our limited comprehension. Thankfully, though, Jesus came to show us how near He really is.
—*Bill Crowder*

Walter Chalmers Smith, who had two doctoral degrees, wrote "Immortal, Invisible" while pastoring a church in Scotland in 1867. He based the song on 1 Timothy 1:17.

HARVEST HOME

Read: James 4:13-17; 5:7-11

You too, be patient and stand firm, because the Lord's coming is near.
—JAMES 5:8

The hymn "Come, Ye Thankful People, Come" is often sung at Christian services of thanksgiving. Written in 1844 by Henry Alford, it begins with thanks to God for crops safely gathered in before winter. But it is more than gratefulness for the bounty of the land. The hymn ends by focusing on God's "harvest" of His people when Christ returns:

*Even so, Lord, quickly come
To Thy final harvest-home:
Gather Thou Thy people in,
Free from sorrow, free from sin;
There, forever purified,
In Thy presence to abide:
Come, with all Thine angels, come—
Raise the glorious harvest-home.*

As we give thanks for material needs supplied, it's essential to remember that our plans are uncertain and our lives are a vapor that quickly disappears (James 4:14). James encourages us to be like a farmer waiting for his crops to grow and mature. "You too, be patient and stand firm, because the Lord's coming is near" (5:8).

As we thank God for His faithful provision for our needs, let's turn our thoughts to the promised return of Jesus Christ. In patient expectation, we live for Him and look for the day when He will come to gather His glorious harvest home.

—*David McCasland*

The man who wrote the music for Henry Alford's words was George Elvey. He was organist for the Royal Chapel at Windsor Castle. In 1871 he was knighted by Queen Victoria.

THANKSGIVING ALL YEAR

Read: 1 Chronicles 16:8-13, 23-36

Give thanks to the LORD, for he is good. —1 CHRONICLES 16:34

The beautiful hymn "We Plow the Fields" is often sung in the United States during the Thanksgiving holiday period in November. For me, it conjures images of families sharing a traditional feast during the harvest season.

But I was surprised when I heard it sung in church during the month of June, far removed from its holiday context. It reminded me that giving thanks to God for His goodness and provision is to be a continuing celebration for His people.

For a special occasion of national celebration, King David wrote a song to guide his people in praising God on that day: "Give praise to the LORD, proclaim his name; make known among the nations what he has done. . . Let the hearts of those who seek the LORD rejoice" (1 Chronicles 16:8, 10). But the song endured as part of Israel's songbook of ongoing praise (Psalm 105:1–15).

Two centuries ago, Matthias Claudius wrote:

We thank Thee, then, O Father, for all things bright and good,
The seedtime and the harvest, our life, our health, our food:
No gifts have we to offer for all Thy love imparts,
But that which Thou desirest, our humble, thankful hearts.
All good gifts around us are sent from heaven above;
Then thank the Lord, O thank the Lord for all His love.

We have so much to be thankful for every day. God continually provides for all our needs. So let's make Thanksgiving a yearlong celebration.

—*David McCasland*

Matthias Claudius, the son of a pastor, was a German poet and editor who died in Hamburg in 1815. He sometimes used the penname "Asmus."

WHAT CHILD IS THIS?

Read: Luke 2:25-35

This child is destined to cause the falling and rising of many in Israel, . . . that the thoughts of many hearts will be revealed. —LUKE 2:34–35

One of our most beloved Christmas carols was written in 1865 by William Dix, an Englishman who managed a maritime insurance company and loved to write hymns. Fashioned after the English melody "Greensleeves," the song is not always sung the same way. Some versions use the latter half of the first verse as a chorus for the other verses:

> *This, this is Christ the King,*
> *Whom shepherds guard and angels sing:*
> *Haste, haste, to bring Him laud—*
> *The Babe, the Son of Mary.*

But in other versions, each stanza is unique. The second verse, rarely sung today, looks beyond the manger to the cross:

> *Why lies He in such mean estate where ox and ass are feeding?*
> *Good Christian, fear—for sinners here the silent Word is pleading.*
> *Nails, spear shall pierce Him through, the cross be borne for me, for you.*
> *Hail, hail the Word made flesh, the Babe, the Son of Mary.*

Simeon said to Mary, "This child is destined to cause the falling and rising of many in Israel, and to be a sign that will be spoken against, so that the thoughts of many hearts will be revealed. And a sword will pierce your own soul too" (Luke 2:34–35).

The Child of Christmas came to be our Savior. "Joy, joy for Christ is born, the Babe, the Son of Mary."

—David McCasland

"What Child Is This?" has been recorded over the years by such stars as Johnny Mathis, the Lettermen, Tony Bennett, Andy Williams, MercyMe, Kevin Max, and Josh Groban.

SOURCE OF GLADNESS

Read: 2 Corinthians 6:3-12

Sorrowful, yet always rejoicing; poor, yet making many rich; having nothing, and yet possessing everything. —2 CORINTHIANS 6:10

Paul Gerhardt, a pastor in Germany during the seventeenth century, had every reason not to be glad. His wife and four of his children died; the Thirty Years' War brought death and devastation across Germany; church conflict and political interference filled his life with distress. Yet despite great personal suffering, he wrote more than 130 hymns, many of them characterized by joy and devotion to Jesus Christ.

One of Gerhardt's hymns, "Holy Spirit, Source of Gladness," contains this verse:

Let that love which knows no measure now in quickening showers descend,
Bringing us the richest treasures man can wish or God can send;
Hear our earnest supplication, every struggling heart release;
Rest upon this congregation, Spirit of untroubled peace.

Because God's abounding love is poured into our hearts by the Holy Spirit (Romans 5:5), is there any situation in which we cannot experience the joy He gives?

During a time of great personal hardship, Paul described his experience as being "sorrowful, yet always rejoicing; poor, yet making many rich; having nothing, and yet possessing everything" (2 Corinthians 6:10).

Pain and sorrow are inescapable facts of life. Yet the Holy Spirit is our source of gladness, "bringing us the richest treasures man can wish or God can send."

—*David McCasland*

In addition to "Holy Spirit," Paul Gerhardt also wrote the famous "O Sacred Head, Now Wounded" based on a Latin poem of the Middle Ages.

EVERLASTING ARMS

Read: Deuteronomy 33:26-29

The eternal God is your refuge, and underneath are the everlasting arms.
—DEUTERONOMY 33:27

After a pre-concert rehearsal in New York City's Carnegie Hall, Randall Atcheson sat on stage alone. He had successfully navigated the intricate piano compositions of Beethoven, Chopin, and Liszt for the evening program, and with only minutes remaining before the doors opened, he wanted to play one more piece for himself. What came from his heart and his hands was an old hymn by Elisha Hoffman:

> *What have I to dread, what have I to fear,*
> *Leaning on the everlasting arms?*

Those words echo the truth in the final blessing of Moses: "There is no one like the God of Jeshurun, who rides across the heavens to help you and on the clouds in his majesty. The eternal God is your refuge, and underneath are the everlasting arms" (Deuteronomy 33:26–27).

What a gift we have in our own arms and hands—they can swing a hammer, hold a child, or help a friend. But while our strength is limited, God's boundless power on our behalf is expressed in might and gentle care. "Surely the arm of the LORD is not too short to save" (Isaiah 59:1). "He gathers the lambs in his arms and carries them close to his heart" (Isaiah 40:11).

Whatever challenge or opportunity we face, there is security and peace in God's everlasting arms.

—David McCasland

Prolific songwriter Elisha Hoffman (1839-1929) wrote more than 2,000 published songs while pastoring churches in Ohio, Michigan, and Illinois. Others include "Down at the Cross," "Have Thine Own Way, Lord," and "Are You Washed in the Blood?"

HE LIVES!

Read: Acts 1:1–10

He presented himself to them and gave many convincing proofs.
—ACTS 1:3

When the World Trade Center towers came crashing to the ground in a deafening roar of billowing debris, citizens of New York experienced what many people in other parts of the world had already known—the fear of terrorism. Subsequent attacks in other countries have heightened the concern that mankind may be spiraling toward self-destruction.

All the unrest in the world might make us think that our future is very bleak. We might even conclude that this is not the kind of world in which to raise children.

Yet one shining hope remains that can brighten our view of the future. Bill Gaither captured it in his song titled "Because He Lives." The idea for this song came to him in the late 1960s, a time of social unrest in the US and conflict in Southeast Asia. His wife Gloria was expecting a child, and they felt that it was a poor time to bring a child into the world. But when their son was born, Bill thought of the living Savior and decided his child could "face uncertain days because He lives."

Two thousand years ago Jesus rose from the grave and gave "many convincing proofs" that He was alive (Acts 1:3). That's why we can keep going in the face of fear. Because Jesus lives, we can face tomorrow.

—*Dave Branon*

———

Before Bill and Gloria Gaither became known worldwide for their uplifting gospel songs and their warm, inviting, down-home style of presentation, they were both schoolteachers. Bill taught English for eight years before he and Gloria (who taught French) went into music full-time. By then, they already had the popular song "He Touched Me" in their repertoire.

WORSHIP

Read: Psalm 150

Let everything that has breath praise the LORD. Praise the LORD.
—PSALM 150:6

Church people can get quite upset about music. Some Christians feel that God is particularly drawn to old hymns sung to the strains of a pipe organ. Others are sure that God enjoys choruses sung over and over again. Some clap their hands when they sing while others fold their arms.

Many modern Christians would be quite unsettled if they had to worship with the ancient Israelites. They might resent the loud, boisterous music. And talk about a praise band! The instruments in the orchestra—wind, string, and percussion together—sounded out their hymns to God. In the middle of the worship, people danced. Large choirs sang their anthems heralding God's greatness. Unfortunately, many Christians would hear only the noise. What is worse, they would be angry because they couldn't fire the worship leader or quit and join another church.

One thing we dare not overlook in our disagreements about worship: God demands our praise! That is not negotiable. There is nothing or no one in the universe more worthy of praise than our Lord himself.

Don't waste your breath arguing about how to worship. Just worship! "Let everything that has breath praise the LORD. Praise the LORD" (Psalm 150:6).

—*Haddon Robinson*

———

According to historians, there have been battles about congregational singing—even including what instruments to use—as far back as the fourth century. At one point in that era, there was a moratorium on congregational singing and the singing was done completely by professional clergy. Congregational singing was reintroduced several hundred years later.

JOY TO THE WORLD

Read: Psalm 98

The LORD has made his salvation known and revealed his righteousness to the nations. —PSALM 98:2

While walking home from a church service in Southampton, England, twenty-year-old Isaac Watts told his father that the metrical psalms sung at their services lacked the dignity and beauty that should characterize hymns used in worship. His father encouraged him to try to create something better. So in the year 1694, Isaac Watts began writing hymns and eventually put the book of Psalms into rhyming meter for worship.

Watts took the prophetic references to the coming Messiah in the Psalms and expressed them in their New Testament fulfillment. His hymns proclaimed that Jesus Christ is Savior and Lord. When Watts came to Psalm 98, he wrote:

> *Joy to the world! The Lord is come!*
> *Let earth receive her King;*
> *Let every heart prepare Him room,*
> *And heaven and nature sing.*
> *Joy to the earth! The Savior reigns!*
> *Let men their songs employ;*
> *While fields and floods, rocks, hills, and plains*
> *Repeat the sounding joy.*

This hymn has become a favorite of the Christmas season. It calls us to acknowledge Christ as Savior and King and to open our hearts to His rule of love and grace.

The psalmist wrote, "Sing to the LORD a new song" (98:1). Isaac Watts did just that in his proclamation that Christ *has* come, and we can rejoice in Him.

—*David McCasland*

Isaac Watts felt the psalms "ought to be translated in such a manner as we have reason to believe David would have composed them if he had lived in our day." This Watts attempted to do in his hymns, combining ideas expressed in the psalms with frequent references to the cross of Christ.

✕

LET IT SHINE

Read: Matthew 5:1–16

Let your light shine before others, that they may see your good deeds and glorify your Father in heaven. —MATTHEW 5:16

As a young boy, I enjoyed singing hymns in church like "Throw Out the Lifeline" and "Let the Lower Lights Be Burning," which used images of shipwreck and danger at sea to illustrate our spiritual responsibility to others. However, living in landlocked Oklahoma I had never seen the ocean, and my nautical experience was limited to sailing Matchbox boats on mud puddles. I knew the words but had little concept of how to rescue a "fainting, struggling seaman."

But in Sunday school, when we sang "This little light of mine, I'm gonna let it shine," it seemed perfectly clear what I should do. Jesus said, "You are the light of the world. . . . Let your light shine before others, that they may see your good deeds and glorify your Father in heaven" (Matthew 5:14, 16). We memorized the Beatitudes (vv. 3–12) as an example of how we could let our lives shine for Him.

As a child I understood that I should not be ashamed to live for Jesus. A secret Christian was like a lamp hidden under a basket instead of shining openly where it could help others (v. 15).

Today, people around us are in spiritual danger and darkness. Young or old, we can let our light shine for Him and for them.

—David McCasland

Henry Dixon Loes's simple song "This Little Light of Mine," written in approximately 1920, has been remixed and rerecorded in many different ways by artists as diverse as Kanye West, Bruce Springsteen, and Ray Charles.

OUR MESSAGE

Read: 1 Corinthians 2:1-8

I resolved to know nothing while I was with you except Jesus Christ and him crucified. —1 CORINTHIANS 2:2

I've heard people say that the Lord sometimes uses simple hymns to impress them with profound truths. Songs like "He Lives," "Great Is Thy Faithfulness," or "Jesus Saves" have jolted them as if they were hearing these truths for the first time.

Something similar happened to me in 1986. I attended a convention that drew 10,000 evangelists from many countries. Our unified concern was to bring God's plan of salvation to our lost and needy world. As I went to seminars and listened to brilliant speakers, I began to wonder if the urgent task of evangelism was beyond me. Then a singer was invited to the platform. My spirit soared with reassurance and confidence as her rich voice proclaimed, "People need the Lord!" She reminded us in song that people all around us need to hear about Jesus and put their faith in Him.

Sharing the gospel means sharing Christ, His death, and His resurrection with people lost in sin. Paul said he didn't minister with eloquence or worldly wisdom. He chose to know nothing "except Jesus Christ and him crucified" (1 Corinthians 2:2).

Yes, there is much knowledge to be learned, but the key to that knowledge is to know the Lord. That's why people need Him. Remember, our message is Christ.

—*Joanie Yoder*

Although Steve Green made "People Need the Lord" famous, it was written by Greg Nelson and Phill McHugh. They came up with the idea while eating at a restaurant and noticing the empty look in the eyes of their waitress. "She needs the Lord," one of them remarked, and the idea was born.

WHEN JESUS COMES IN

Read: Mark 5:1-20

Daughter, your faith has healed you. Go in peace and be freed from your suffering. —MARK 5:34

In 1932, as the United States was undergoing a financial breakdown, missionary Robert Cummings was suffering an emotional breakdown. As he carried on his evangelistic ministry with his wife in India, he became obsessed by blasphemous and sinful thoughts so overwhelming that he felt cast aside by God and eternally lost. Hospital care and therapy were of no help. His wife brought him back to the US where he was placed in a private mental facility.

For two more years Robert underwent indescribable emotional agony. Then one morning he knelt beside his bed begging for relief. God answered dramatically with the words of a poem by James Procter:

My soul is night, my heart is steel—I cannot see, I cannot feel;
For light, for life, I must appeal in simple faith to Jesus.

As Robert repeated those lines, peace surged through his soul. Dread vanished from his heart and he was filled with joy and gratitude. Then a hymn by William Sleeper welled up from the depths of his memory, which he sang with one significant change. For him it wasn't, "Jesus, I come to Thee," but "Jesus has come to me."

—*Vernon Grounds*

William Sleeper's commission in life was to start churches. He planted three churches in Maine and one in Massachusetts. Eventually, he met a song leader named George Stebbins. The two collaborated on the song "Ye Must Be Born Again." Later, when Sleeper had written the words for "Jesus, I Come," he called on Stebbins to help him with the music—and another song was born.

FRIENDSHIP WITH JESUS

Read: John 15:9-17

You are my friends if you do what I command. —JOHN 15:14

Joseph Scriven (1819–1886), writer of the much-loved hymn "What a Friend We Have in Jesus," knew the pain of heartache and loneliness. His bride-to-be drowned the evening before their wedding. Later a second fiancée died of pneumonia, and again his hopes for marriage were dashed. Yet Christ's friendship sustained him.

Anyone can have that same comforting friendship. At one point in my life, I came to know John, a recovering addict who at the lowest point in his life put his faith in Jesus. He sensed that the Lord was asking him, "Do you want a friend forever?" As John wept over his broken condition, he sobbed, "Yes," and Christ came into his life.

Later, John told me that he urgently needed a liver transplant. "You know, John," I said, "cynical people might say, 'Some friend Jesus has turned out to be, considering your condition.' " John replied, "But *I'm* not saying that." Then he added, "I certainly don't want to leave my family. But however it goes, Jesus remains my friend."

In John 15:14, Jesus said that we are *His* friends, suggesting that this is a two-way relationship. But He added one important condition: We must walk obediently with Him. Only then can we testify, "Whatever happens, Jesus remains my friend."

—*Joanie Yoder*

Born in Ireland, Joseph Scriven moved to Canada, where he led a life of restraint and poverty—given to share all he had with people in need.

THE WONDROUS CROSS

Read: John 19:14-30

Carrying his own cross, [Jesus] went out to the place of the Skull (which in Aramaic is called Golgotha). There they crucified him.
—JOHN 19:17–18

Mahatma Gandhi asked some missionaries who visited him during one of his numerous fasts to sing a hymn for him. "Which hymn?" they asked. "The one that expresses all that is deepest in your faith," he replied. They thought for a moment and then sang these words written by Isaac Watts:

> *When I survey the wondrous cross*
> *On which the Prince of glory died,*
> *My richest gain I count but loss,*
> *And pour contempt on all my pride.*

Yes, there is something wondrous about the cross that stirs our hearts. When we think back to Calvary, our souls are saddened and yet thrilled with the wonder of it all. With heartfelt gratitude we exclaim, "Thank you, Lord, for saving my soul!"

When George Briggs was governor of Massachusetts in the mid-1800s, three of his friends visited the Holy Land. While they were there, they climbed Golgotha's slope and cut from the hilltop a stick to be used as a cane. On their return they presented it to the governor, saying, "We want you to know that when we stood on Calvary, we thought of you." He accepted the gift with gratitude and then remarked, "I appreciate your consideration of me, gentlemen, but I am still more thankful for Another who thought of me there!"

Yes, Jesus thought of you and me when hanging there in agony. A life of gratitude would be our appropriate response. With Isaac Watts we can say, "Love so amazing, so divine, demands my soul, my life, my all."

—*Henry Bosch*

At the time Isaac Watts wrote "When I Survey the Wondrous Cross" in 1707, the tradition was for the church to sing songs with lyrics taken exclusively from Scripture—especially the Old Testament. This song departed from that pattern, yet it was well accepted.

)X(

A UNIQUE CHOIR

Read: Romans 15:5-13

That with one mind and one voice you may glorify the God and Father of our Lord Jesus Christ. —ROMANS 15:6

When Mitch Miller died in July 2010, most people remembered him as the man who invited everyone to sing along. On his popular 1960s TV program *Sing Along with Mitch,* an all-male chorus sang well-loved songs while the words appeared on the screen so viewers could join in. A *Los Angeles Times* obituary cited Miller's belief that one reason for the program's success was the appeal of his chorus: "I always made a point of hiring singers who were tall, short, bald, round, fat, whatever—everyday-looking guys." From that unified diversity came beautiful music in which everyone was invited to participate.

In Romans 15, Paul called for unity among the followers of Christ—"that with one mind and one voice you may glorify the God and Father of our Lord Jesus Christ" (v. 6). From several Old Testament passages, he spoke of Gentiles and Jews together singing praise to God (vv. 9–12). A unity that had been considered impossible became reality as people who had been deeply divided began thanking God together for His mercy shown in Christ. Like them, we are filled with joy, peace, and hope "by the power of the Holy Spirit" (v. 13).

What a unique "choir" we belong to, and what a privilege it is to sing along!

—*David McCasland*

Each congregation comprises its own unique choir—allowing singers and non-singers alike the anonymity of singing praises together to God. In the Bible, perhaps one of the first choirs was the children of Israel as they sang the Song of Moses found in Exodus 15:1-18.

GOD REIGNS

Read: Psalm 46

The LORD reigns, let the earth be glad. —PSALM 97:1

In Germany in the late 1930s, young Dr. Herbert Gezork was fortunate that he was sentenced to exile instead of execution. Yet the night before his departure for America, he wandered the streets of Hamburg in deep despair. He kept asking, "What hope is there in a world where demonic forces are triumphing?"

Then Gezork heard music coming from a church. He walked in and listened as the organist played Martin Luther's hymn "A Mighty Fortress Is Our God." The words of one stanza came to mind:

And though this world, with devils filled, should threaten to undo us,
We will not fear, for God hath willed His truth to triumph through us.

Gradually the truth of the lyrics sank into Dr. Gerzork's soul and brought him peace.

The words of Psalm 46 can do the same for us in times of despair. The psalmist declares God's mastery over the forces of nature (vv. 1–3) and His triumph over the nations (vv. 4–10). The Lord will judge the wicked and rescue His people. To the restless and rebellious He says, "Be still, and know that I am God; . . . I will be exalted in the earth!" (v. 10). We who know Him can joyfully exclaim, "The LORD Almighty is with us; the God of Jacob is our fortress" (v. 11). Our God reigns!

—Herb Vander Lugt

Written in his native German by Martin Luther in the late 1520s, "A Mighty Fortress Is Our God" was first translated into English in 1539 by Myles Coverdale, a noted Bible translator. The translation we sing today was penned in 1853 by Frederick Hedge.

TIME TO PRAISE

Read: Psalm 30

You turned my wailing into dancing. —PSALM 30:11

It was the worst of times. In the first half of the seventeenth century, Germany was in the midst of wars and famine and pestilence. In the city of Eilenburg lived a pastor by the name of Martin Rinkart (1586–1649).

During one especially oppressive period, Rinkart conducted up to fifty funerals a day as a plague swept through the town and as the Thirty Years' War wreaked its own terror on the people. Among those whom Rinkart buried were members of his own family.

Yet during those years of darkness and despair, when death and destruction greeted each new day, Pastor Rinkart wrote sixty-six sacred songs and hymns. Among them was the song "Now Thank We All Our God." As sorrow crouched all around him, Rinkart wrote:

> *Now thank we all our God with hearts and hands and voices,*
> *Who wondrous things hath done, in whom His world rejoices;*
> *Who from our mothers' arms hath blessed us on our way*
> *With countless gifts of love, and still is ours today.*

Rinkart demonstrated a valuable lesson for us all: Thankfulness does not have to wait for prosperity and peace. It's always a good time to praise God for the "wondrous things" He has done.

—Dave Branon

In addition to the plague, Eilenburg also suffered through a severe famine and even monetary abuse from high government taxes. Yet Martin Rinkart gave of everything he had to help his people and to remind them to be grateful.

WORTHY OF PRAISE

Read: Psalm 150

Praise him for his surpassing greatness. —PSALM 150:2

A well-known theologian was asked to explain the gospel. In response, he simply quoted from a children's hymn, "Jesus loves me! This I know, for the Bible tells me so."

The great truths of our faith can be expressed in very simple terms, such as "God is love" or "Christ died for our sins and rose again." They can also be expressed in profound doctrines and propositions.

In the end, however, the truth about our infinite God is beyond human understanding and expression. As Paul exclaimed, "How unsearchable his judgments, and his paths beyond tracing out!" (Romans 11:33). Sometimes all we can do is praise our Lord for His greatness with our words and with our songs (Psalm 150:2).

The psalmist talked about using all kinds of instruments in praise and worship of the Lord (vv. 3–5). We too use hymns, choruses, cantatas, organs, pianos, orchestras, and every available form of music to convey our adoration of the God "who alone is immortal and who lives in unapproachable light" (1 Timothy 6:16).

God has revealed himself so we can know Him and the salvation He provides. But we will never understand the depth of His being. He is worthy of all praise!

—Vernon Grounds

The theologian in question in this story is Karl Barth, and the truthfulness of the story has been verified by people who were at the event when he made the statement.

THE DANGER OF DENIAL

Read: John 18:12-27

If we endure, we will also reign with him. If we disown him,
he will also disown us. —2 TIMOTHY 2:12

We usually think that denying Christ is an outright act—like Peter's disavowal of Jesus in John 18. But Reginald Heber (1783–1826), the English writer of the hymn "Holy, Holy, Holy," pointed out that we can deny the Savior in more subtle ways.

Heber wrote: "We deny our Lord whenever, like Demas, we, through love of this present world, forsake the course of duty which Christ has plainly pointed out to us. We deny our Lord whenever we lend . . . our praise, or even our silence, to [things] . . . which we ourselves believe to be sinful. . . . We deny our Lord whenever we forsake a good man in affliction, and refuse to give countenance, encouragement, and support to those who, for God's sake and for the faithful discharge of their duty, are exposed to persecutions and slander."

Those who have been born again will consciously avoid any open, deliberate, and vocal denial of the Lord. But loving the world, failing to do as God directs, tolerating sin, and refusing to support our fellow believers are subtle ways we do, in effect, deny the One who has redeemed us.

Let's determine to live faithfully for Jesus so that no one will ever be able to accuse us of turning our backs on Him. Remember, we're always in danger of denial.

—*Richard DeHaan*

Reginald Heber's hymns, including "Holy, Holy, Holy," were published after his death in India. He had gone to India in 1823 with his young family to be a missionary.

✕

ONE TONGUE IS ENOUGH

Read: Psalm 45

My tongue is the pen of a skillful writer. —PSALM 45:1

All of us as Christians who long to proclaim the riches of Christ and His good news know the limitations of having only one tongue. In one of his hymns, Charles Wesley (1707–1788) wrote, "O for a thousand tongues to sing my great Redeemer's praise!"

The fact is, though, that our one tongue has vastly greater potential than most of us will ever put to use. A tongue devoted to God can accomplish much.

For example, a man from Chicago was blind and had neither arms nor legs. But like the psalmist, his heart was overflowing with God's love, and his tongue was fully dedicated for His use. This man learned to read the Braille Bible using his tongue! As a result of this painstaking accomplishment, he was able to use his tongue in a different way—to teach the Word of God and to share his radiant testimony.

Joni Eareckson Tada, another believer with physical disabilities, has spoken to millions about Christ. She often affirms, "With God, less is more."

Are you sometimes discouraged, thinking that you have little to offer to God? If you have Christ's love in your heart and a willing tongue in your mouth, offer them boldly to God today and begin to bring praise and honor to the Lord. One tongue is enough.

—*Joanie Yoder*

Charles Wesley wrote 6,000 hymns during his lifetime. He wrote "O for a Thousand Tongues" in 1739. During his years of writing, he tried to pen three hymns a week.

THE WITNESS OF SUFFERING

Read: Acts 7:54-8:4

Those who had been scattered preached the word wherever they went.
—ACTS 8:4

How do we lead people to choose Christ? The use of logic, or apologetics, is one way. But we will probably get a lot further by living an active, unwavering faith before them.

Consider the witness we give when we are faithful through suffering. My mind is drawn to Annie Johnson Flint, author of thousands of hymns and gospel songs. Her birth parents died when she was very young. She lived with crippling arthritis. She was stricken with cancer. Yet her faith was especially evident in this hymn:

> *He giveth more grace when the burdens grow greater,*
> *He sendeth more strength when the labors increase;*
> *To added afflictions He addeth His mercy,*
> *To multiplied trials His multiplied peace.*

God has a remarkable way of using negative circumstances to bring about good. The persecution of the early church, while intended to stamp out the gospel, actually resulted in its rapid growth (Acts 8:4). And though no one would call the suffering of Annie Johnson Flint a good thing, her faithfulness through trials was a wonderful witness to God's grace.

May our faithfulness in the midst of suffering be used to deliver a powerful witness for Christ.

—David Egner

Annie Johnson Flint spent most of her adult life in a sanatorium as she battled debilitating arthritis. A teacher by profession, she had to give that up because of her physical disabilities.

GRANDPA'S LAST HYMN

Read: Matthew 26:17-30

When they had sung a hymn, they went out to the Mount of Olives.
—MATTHEW 26:30

As our Lord faced the terrible prospect of dying on the cross, He concluded the first Communion service with the singing of a hymn. By this He showed that believers can meet the "last enemy" with peaceful confidence when they have faith in God.

I remember hearing my parents telling about Grandpa Bosch's final moments on this earth. He had become afflicted with a serious heart ailment, and in spite of the doctor's best efforts to relieve his condition he steadily worsened. Calling his children to his side, he lovingly spoke to each of them. Then he said, "Let's part with a hymn." His weak voice quavered as he sang these familiar words by Edward Mote:

> *My hope is built on nothing less*
> *Than Jesus' blood and righteousness.*
> *His oath, His covenant, His blood,*
> *Support me in the whelming flood.*
> *When all around my soul gives way,*
> *He then is all my hope and stay.*
> *On Christ, the solid Rock, I stand,*
> *All other ground is sinking sand.*

After a tender word of spiritual admonition, Grandpa closed his eyes and went to be with the Lord.

If we rely on Christ, we too will have that kind of peace when we come to the end of our lives.

—Henry Bosch

On the day Edward Mote wrote "On Christ the Solid Rock," he was asked to visit a woman who was very ill. He took the poem with him and sang it to her. Later that day he added two more verses and made copies for distribution. That was 1836.

SAFE IN GOD'S CARE

Read: Acts 27:27-44

*The LORD will watch over your coming and going both now
and forevermore.* —PSALM 121:8

President Franklin D. Roosevelt loved the song we call the "Navy Hymn." It was sung at his funeral in Hyde Park, New York, on April 14, 1945. The words of the hymn were written in 1860 by Englishman William Whiting, who directed a sixteen-voice boys choir. He penned them for a student who was about to set sail for America and who was apprehensive about the journey.

The tune was written by John B. Dykes and first published in 1861. He named the hymn tune "Melita," the Roman name for Malta, the island where Paul was shipwrecked.

The hymn is a simple prayer based on the profound truth that the eternal God who created the universe controls all the elements of nature and can protect His own no matter how great the peril. Wind and wave are subject to His command.

Eternal Father, strong to save,
Whose arm doth bind the restless wave,
Who bidd'st the mighty ocean deep
Its own appointed limits keep;
O hear us when we cry to Thee
For those in peril on the sea!

When we or loved ones take a journey to some far-off destination, or if we only travel to and from work, we can think of these famous words from this widely respected hymn and be sure of God's protection and care.

—*David Egner*

In 1879, Rear Admiral Charles Jackson Train began the tradition of ending the worship service on Sunday at the US Naval Academy with a singing of the first verse of the "Navy Hymn."

ALWAYS AVAILABLE

Read: 2 Corinthians 12:7–10

I can do all this through him who gives me strength.
—PHILIPPIANS 4:13

Swedish hymnist Lina Sandell Berg (1832–1903) served with her father in an evangelistic ministry. As they were traveling by boat across Lake Vattern in their homeland, he accidentally fell overboard and drowned. In need of the comfort that only God can supply, Lina wrote the following words that are still sung by Christians around the world:

Day by day and with each passing moment,
Strength I find to meet my trials here;
Trusting in my Father's wise bestowment,
I've no cause for worry or for fear.

Secular counselors advise us to draw strength from our own inner resources. But that's hopelessly unrealistic. The simple fact is that in and of ourselves we don't have what it takes to deal with all of life's pressures and problems. Even the strongest among us have weaknesses. We're susceptible to vacillating moods, sinful temptations, and enslaving habits.

In 2 Corinthians 12:7–10, the apostle Paul referred to a weakness he called a "thorn in the flesh." But he didn't tough it out on his own. He prayed for deliverance, but instead of getting that, he was strengthened by the Lord so he could endure his overwhelming difficulties.

In times of conflict and defeat, we are forced to confess that we need a source of strength beyond ourselves. And we can rejoice that there's an always-available source on which we can draw—the inexhaustible grace of God.

—*Vernon Grounds*

It has been noted that "Day by Day" and other songs Lina wrote following her father's death were instrumental in fueling a revival that touched thousands of lives in Scandinavia in the later half of the nineteenth century.

CHURCH COMPETITION

Read: Philippians 1:12-18

Whether from false motives or true, Christ is preached. And because of this I rejoice. —PHILIPPIANS 1:18

Three churches, located on different corners of the same intersection, didn't get along. One Sunday each of them opened their meeting with a rousing song service. It was a warm day and all the doors and windows were wide open. One congregation began singing the old hymn, "Will There Be Any Stars in My Crown?" The strains had barely faded away when the congregation across the street started singing, "No, Not One, No, Not One!" They had scarcely finished when the third church began singing, "Oh, That Will Be Glory for Me."

Of course, this is just a humorous story, but it reminds us that a spirit of divisive competition does exist among some churches. Naturally, we will want to support our own church, pray for it, and rejoice in its growth. But we must never feel self-satisfied or be critical of churches that have problems or are not growing.

If there is a place for "competition," let it be to oppose those who deny scriptural fundamentals and the gospel. But if a church is true to God's Word and is winning people to Christ, regardless of its label, let's rejoice. That should be our attitude when faced with the competitive motives of envy and strife. Let's avoid church competition.

—*Richard DeHaan*

The song "Oh, That Will Be Glory for Me" is sometimes called the "Glory Song." It has faced criticism from some because of its over-emphasis on the believer's heavenly reward bringing glory to us instead of to God.

TELL IT TO JESUS

Read: Matthew 14:1-12

John's disciples came and took his body and buried it. Then they went and told Jesus. —MATTHEW 14:12

When I was a young boy, a neighbor who lived two doors from us suffered a terrible tragedy. She often played and sang at her piano, but after her great sorrow the first song she always sang when she sat down to play was "I Must Tell Jesus." The words of that lovely old hymn made a deep impression on me.

> *I must tell Jesus all of my troubles,*
> *He is a kind, compassionate Friend;*
> *If I but ask Him, He will deliver,*
> *Make of my troubles quickly an end.*
> *I must tell Jesus! I must tell Jesus!*
> *I cannot bear these burdens alone;*
> *I must tell Jesus! I must tell Jesus!*
> *Jesus can help me, Jesus alone.*

I learned later that God answered our neighbor's prayers in such unusual ways that out of her sorrows came great blessings. Apparently, Jesus had become more real to her than He had ever been before her terrible tragedy.

Matthew said that after John the Baptist was beheaded his disciples "took his body and buried it" (14:12). The record is strangely silent about any sorrow, but the last part of the verse says it all. Matthew wrote that they "went and told Jesus." It seemed the only thing to do. Are you heavy-hearted? Tell it to Jesus!

—*Henry Bosch*

Pastor Elisha Hoffman (see "Everlasting Arms") visited a parishioner who faced many struggles. She asked Pastor Hoffman what to do, and he said she should tell Jesus her troubles. She responded, "I must tell Jesus, I must tell Jesus." Later that day, with those words in his head, Hoffman wrote the song.

JUST AS YOU ARE

Read: Titus 2:11–3:5

*For it is by grace you have been saved, through faith—and this is not from
yourselves, it is the gift of God—not by works, so that no one can boast.*
—EPHESIANS 2:8–9

Cesar Malan (1787–1864), a famous minister from Geneva,
Switzerland, had a genuine interest in the spiritual welfare of
anyone with whom he came in contact. On one occasion, after
being introduced to a woman, Malan asked his new acquaintance about her personal relationship with the Lord. Caught
off guard, and somewhat annoyed by his question, she curtly
said that she didn't care to discuss the matter. The minister
kindly assured her that he would be praying for her salvation.

It wasn't long before circumstances brought the two together
again. As they talked, it became apparent to Pastor Malan
that his prayers were being answered. The once antagonistic
woman had recognized her spiritual need and was now asking
him what was required to come to the Savior. The preacher
replied, "Come to Him just as you are." And that's what she
did. Realizing that she could do nothing to save herself and
depending on the finished work of Christ on the cross to pay
for her sins, she received Him by faith as her Savior. That
woman was Charlotte Elliott, who later wrote the beloved
hymn, "Just As I Am."

All who desire to be saved must come to the Lord Jesus the
same way she did. Admitting their sinfulness, and believing
that Christ died for them, they must trust Him and Him alone
for their salvation. Have you ever done that? If not, right now
make the words of Charlotte Elliott your prayer.

—*Richard DeHaan*

Cesar Malan was a renaissance man, of sorts, not long after the
Renaissance. He was a pastor, a songwriter, a writer, an artist, and
a mechanic. But most of all, he loved to share the gospel.

"JUST AS I AM"

Read: John 6:35-40

All those the Father gives me will come to me, and whoever comes to me I will never drive away. —JOHN 6:37

Charlotte Elliott (1789–1871) learned an important lesson about Jesus one sleepless night in 1834. Some time after her salvation (see "Just As You Are"), she became disabled and was unable to attend when her family held a bazaar in Brighton, England, to raise money to build a school.

That night she was overwhelmed by her inability to help, and she could not sleep. But her sadness was turned to joy when she recalled that God accepted her just as she was.

That experience inspired her to write:

> *Just as I am, without one plea*
> *But that Thy blood was shed for me,*
> *And that Thou bidd'st me come to Thee,*
> *O Lamb of God, I come! I come!*

Jesus always accepts people as they are. In John 6, the people had come from miles around to hear Jesus. When the crowd became hungry, He miraculously fed them with a boy's unselfish gift of five loaves and two fish. Then the Lord offered himself as "the bread of life," promising that He would not turn away anyone who came to Him.

It's still true today. No one who comes to Jesus will be turned away. Come to Him with all your sin—just as you are. Our Savior's salvation, purchased with His death on the cross, can make you just as you should be.

—*David Egner*

Charlotte Elliott wrote "Just as I Am" when she was 45 years old, and the words were first published in 1836. The music we associate with the hymn was written in 1849 by William B. Bradbury.

FRUIT—AFTER MANY DAYS!

Read: Ecclesiastes 11:1-6

That person is like a tree planted by streams of water, which yields its fruit in season and whose leaf does not wither—whatever they do prospers.
—PSALM 1:3

In the previous two devotions, you read the story of how Charlotte Elliott came to write her heart-searching hymn "Just As I Am." Miss Elliott suffered intense pain in her bedridden condition, and she was seldom permitted a visitor. Those who looked at her life may have thought it was wasted, but after her death, friends found in an old trunk more than 1,000 letters that had come to her from all over the world, thanking her for the courage, inspiration, and comfort her one simple invitation song had brought to them.

Like a well-watered tree of the Lord, she had done His bidding and brought forth "much fruit," although it was not until "after many days" that it became evident how much the Lord had prospered her in penning her beloved and immortal hymn.

I am sure that someday many more thousands will testify in glory that "Just As I Am" was used of the Lord to bring the conviction of heart and understanding of mind that was needed to usher them into the kingdom of God!

If our "leaf of testimony" does not wither, we, like Charlotte Elliott, will yield "fruit" in God's appointed "season"—even though it may be after many days!

—*Henry Bosch*

William B. Bradbury, who wrote the music for Charlotte Elliott's "Just As I Am," also wrote the tunes that accompany "He Leadeth Me," "Sweet Hour of Prayer," and "Savior, Like a Shepherd Lead Us."

✕

"O YES, HE CARES"

Read: Luke 12:22-30

Cast all your anxiety on him because he cares for you. —1 PETER 5:7

Sometimes Christians wonder if God really cares. These periods of questioning usually do not arise during happier times. Instead, they occur when the burdens of life weigh heavily, when temptation has been overpowering, or when a final farewell must be said. Yet our text for today says the Lord Jesus cares so much that He will always be with us to help.

A hymn on this theme, "Does Jesus Care?" by Frank E. Graeff (1860–1919), has brought comfort to thousands. In his book *101 More Hymn Stories*, Kenneth Osbeck wrote, "Mr. Graeff was a pastor in the Philadelphia area. Throughout the district, he was known as 'the sunshine minister.' C. Austin Miles, author of the popular hymn, 'In the Garden,' paid this tribute to Mr. Graeff: 'He is a spiritual optimist, a great friend of children; his bright sun-shining disposition attracts him not only to children, but to all with whom he comes in contact. He has a holy magnetism and a childlike faith.' In spite of his cheery disposition and winsome personality, Graeff was often called upon to go through severe testing experiences." While enduring one such test—he faced severe despondency, doubt, and physical agony—Graeff turned to the Scriptures for solace and strength. The words of 1 Peter 5:7, "he cares for you," spoke deeply to him, and the hymn "Does Jesus Care?" was born.

Is your heart filled with pain or grief? Read 1 Peter 5:7 and remind yourself, "O yes, He cares!"

—David Egner

Frank E. Graeff was not just a songwriter (200 songs) and a pastor; he was also a novelist. His book was called *The Minister's Twins*.

THE CLEANSING BLOOD

Read: 1 John 1

If we walk in the light, as he is in the light, we have fellowship with one another, and the blood of Jesus, his Son, purifies us from all sin.
—1 JOHN 1:7

The hymns of Frances Ridley Havergal have greatly blessed the church. She wrote such songs as "Who Is on the Lord's Side?" "Like a River Glorious," "I Gave My Life for Thee," and "Take My Life and Let It Be." She was not always a happy Christian, however. As F. J. Huegel pointed out in his book *Forever Triumphant*, she was perhaps overly sensitive to faults in her life and a defeated believer. Huegel says, "She walked with bowed head. Romans 7 seemed to be her lot."

One day, though, she had a life-transforming experience. Huegel says that the Lord led her into the joy and blessing described in Romans 8. A great crisis marked Havergal's entrance into "the promised land of a life of fullness and victory." She was reading her New Testament in the Greek, as she often did. When she came to 1 John 1:7, she discovered from the tense of the verb that the blood of Christ *keeps on* cleansing the believer who walks in the light. Says Huegel, "The result for Frances Havergal was a mighty revolution. A new day dawned. She would no longer be sad because of her faults and blemishes. She would rejoice because of the infinite efficacy of the Savior's atoning death."

As we journey through this sinful world, we become defiled. But thank God, the blood of Jesus Christ *keeps on* cleansing us from all sin.

—*Richard DeHaan*

Not only did Frances Havergal read Greek, but she also learned Latin and Hebrew. She memorized the Psalms, Isaiah, and most of the New Testament during her 43 years of life. First John 1:7 was engraved on her tombstone in Swansea, Wales.

HIS LOVE, NOT OURS

Read: 1 John 4:7-16

So the sisters sent word to Jesus, "Lord, the one you love is sick."
—JOHN 11:3

When a godly Christian became seriously ill, several friends gathered around his bedside to ask God to restore him. The last one to pray spoke of the faithful service of this man and concluded his petition by saying, "Lord, You know how he loves You." After a moment of silence, the sick believer said to him, "I know you meant well, but please don't plead for my recovery on that basis. When Lazarus was ill, Mary and Martha sent for Jesus, but their request was not based on his affection for Christ. They said, 'Lord, he whom You love is sick.' It's not my weak and faltering allegiance to Him that calls forth His attention but His perfect love for me that is my constant strength and hope."

The same thought was forcefully impressed on hymn writer Philip P. Bliss one day after he finished singing "Oh, How I Love Jesus." "These words are true," he said. "Yet I feel guilty for having sung so much about my poor love for Christ and so little about His endless love for me." As a result, he wrote a song that is well known today. It reads,

> *I am so glad that our Father in heaven*
> *Tells of His love in the Book He has given,*
> *Wonderful things in the Bible I see—*
> *This is the dearest, that Jesus loves me.*

Yes, our greatest comfort in life or in death is not that we love Him, but that "he loved us" (1 John 4:10).

—*Henry Bosch*

Philip P. Bliss died at the age of 38 while traveling by train near Ashtabula, Ohio. He and his wife both died when a bridge collapsed and the train crashed into a ravine on December 29, 1876.

ONE LAST SONG

Read: Hebrews 13:7-17

Keep your lives free from the love of money and be content with what you have, because God has said, "Never will I leave you; never will I forsake you." —HEBREWS 13:5

Renowned pastor Louis Albert Banks (1855–1933) tells of an elderly Christian man, a fine singer, who learned that he had cancer of the tongue and that surgery was required. In the hospital, the man asked the doctor, "Do you think I will ever sing again?" The surgeon found it difficult to answer his question. He simply shook his head no. The patient then asked if he could sit up for a moment. "I've had many good times singing the praises of God," he said. "And now you tell me I can never sing again. I have one song that will be my last. It will be of gratitude and praise to God." There in the doctor's presence the man sang softly the words of Isaac Watts' hymn,

> *I'll praise my Maker while I've breath,*
> *And when my voice is lost in death,*
> *Praise shall employ my nobler powers;*
> *My days of praise shall ne'er be past,*
> *While life, and thought, and being last,*
> *Or immortality endures.*

Praise in times of trial isn't natural—it's the supernatural work of the Holy Spirit in the heart of an obedient believer. It doesn't have to be expressed in the beautiful lines of a hymn, nor sung with a lovely voice. It can be the simple testimony of a grateful heart that says, "Though I have little or nothing, thank God I have Jesus. What more could I ask!"

—Dennis DeHaan

According to the journal of eighteenth-century theologian John Wesley, in an entry written "by one who was present," this was the last song he sang from his deathbed in March 1791.

"JESUS, SAVIOR, PILOT ME"

Read: Matthew 8:23-27

He stilled the storm to a whisper; the waves of the sea were hushed. They
were glad when it grew calm, and he guided them to their desired haven.
—PSALM 107:29–30

One of the most vivid pictures of the Christian's journey through life is that of a voyage on a storm-tossed sea. Edward Hopper (1818–1888) captured this theme in his well-loved hymn "Jesus, Savior, Pilot Me." Born and raised on America's East Coast, he knew much about the sea. For 17 years he pastored a church that was originally established as a mission for sailors and fishermen. Hopper loved these men and was intrigued by their accounts of harrowing experiences during storms and high winds. After preaching one Sunday from Matthew 8, the account of Jesus calming the boisterous Sea of Galilee, he felt inspired to write the words of his now famous hymn. The last stanza is beautiful in its simplicity and directness:

When at last I near the shore,
And the fearful breakers roar
'Twixt me and the peaceful rest—
Then, while leaning on Thy breast,
May I hear Thee say to me, "Fear not—I will pilot thee!"

Hopper knew the reality of those words in his own life. Several years after writing that song, he composed another bit of verse about heaven. After Hopper died, he was found in his study chair, pencil still in hand—with that unfinished poem about heaven on the paper in front of him. In a real sense he experienced the answer to the closing line of the prayer expressed years before: "May I hear Thee say to me, 'Fear not—I will pilot thee.' "

Friend, only when Jesus is at the helm of your life will you arrive safely at the "desired haven" of heaven.

—Henry Bosch

According to legend, the day before Edward Hopper died, he preached on this verse: "Watch ye therefore, for ye know neither the day nor the hour wherein the Son of Man cometh."

GLORY IN THE CROSS!

Read: John 19:16-30

May I never boast except in the cross of our Lord Jesus Christ, through which the world has been crucified to me, and I to the world.
—GALATIANS 6:14

At a gospel meeting I was privileged to hear George Bennard sing "The Old Rugged Cross." Before singing that favorite of all hymns, he told the audience that the inspiration to write it came to him one day in 1913. He said, "After composing the melody, the words were put into my heart in answer to my own need in a time of crisis. I had come to realize that the cross is more than just a religious symbol. Along with the resurrection, it is at the very heart of the gospel."

Following that brief introduction, Mr. Bennard sang "The Old Rugged Cross" as I had never heard it rendered before. When he came to the second verse, his heart seemed to be gripped anew by the stirring message of the Savior's sacrifice, and tears began flowing down his cheeks as he sang,

> *O that old rugged cross, so despised by the world,*
> *Has a wondrous attraction for me;*
> *For the dear Lamb of God left His glory above*
> *To bear it to dark Calvary.*
> *To the old rugged cross I will ever be true,*
> *Its shame and reproach gladly bear;*
> *Then He'll call me someday to my home far away,*
> *Where His glory forever I'll share.*

May we never be ashamed of what Jesus did for us. Let us glory in that old rugged cross, where the "dearest and best" suffered and died for unworthy rebels like you and me.

—*Henry Bosch*

———

Reed City, Michigan, where Bennard lived, is the home of the Old Rugged Cross Historical Museum.

A GREAT AND
GRAND REUNION

Read: 1 Thessalonians 4:13-18

We who are still alive and are left will be caught up together with them in
the clouds to meet the Lord in the air. —1 THESSALONIANS 4:17

In a sermon about heaven, evangelist D. L. Moody (1837–1899) told about fishermen who ventured far out upon the Adriatic Sea off the east coast of Italy. Toward evening their wives would go down to the seashore to await the reunion with their husbands. Standing there, they would sing the first verse of a hymn. Then they would listen till they heard the second verse, carried by the wind across the waves, sung by those men. Moody would continue, "Perhaps if we would listen, we too might hear on this storm-tossed world of ours, some sound, some whisper borne from loved ones afar." Of course, Moody knew that Christians who die are "at home with the Lord" (2 Corinthians 5:8). Yet, as he contemplated being united with them someday, he said he could almost hear the echo of their voices.

Most of us have dear ones in heaven. I like to think that even as we long to see them, they are eagerly awaiting that day when we'll all be together again. No doubt Fanny Crosby had this in mind when she wrote:

O the friends that now are waiting, in the cloudless realms of day,
Who are calling me to follow where their steps have led the way;
I shall see them, I shall know them, I shall hear their song of love,
And we'll all sing hallelujah in our Father's house above.

One of these days, whether we pass through death's valley or meet our loved ones in the air, we're going to have a great and grand reunion.

—*Richard DeHaan*

Interestingly, Fanny Crosby, who was blind from infancy, entitled the song mentioned above "The Blessed Lights of Home."

"NEARER, MY GOD, TO THEE"

Read: James 4:1-8

Come near to God and he will come near to you. Wash your hands, you sinners, and purify your hearts, you double-minded. —JAMES 4:8

Sarah Flower Adams (1805–1848) of England was known for her literary talents. One day her pastor said he wished he could find a song to use with his sermon about the Lord's unique appearance to Jacob recorded in Genesis 28. In that passage Jacob was reminded of God's covenant of grace with him through a dream, which drew him into a closer fellowship with God. Having caught the gist of her minister's sermon, Sarah skillfully condensed that biblical story into five stanzas. These two give the spiritual flavor of its lyrics:

> *Nearer, my God, to Thee, nearer to Thee!*
> *E'en though it be a cross that raiseth me;*
> *Still all my song shall be, nearer, my God, to Thee.*
> *Nearer, my God, to Thee, nearer to Thee!*
> *There let the way appear, steps unto heaven;*
> *All that Thou sendest me, in mercy given—*
> *Angels to beckon me nearer, my God, to Thee.*

Many stories have been told of how this song was used in the hour of crisis. William McKinley, assassinated American president, whispered some of its words on his deathbed on September 14, 1901. And according to legend, in 1912 as the *Titanic* sank into the Atlantic sending 1,500 people into eternity, survivors said the band played "Nearer, My God, to Thee."

The theme of this hymn ought to be our heart's desire today.

—*Henry Bosch*

The song "Nearer, My God, to Thee" was played at the funerals of US presidents James Garfield, Warren G. Harding, and Gerald R. Ford.

EVERYONE SINGS!

Read: Revelation 5:8-14

To him who sits on the throne and to the Lamb be praise and honor and glory and power, for ever and ever! —REVELATION 5:13

Each summer I enjoy attending many of the outdoor concerts presented in our city. During one performance by a brass band, several of the members briefly introduced themselves and told how much they enjoyed practicing and playing together.

The pleasure of sharing music in community has drawn people together for centuries. As followers of Christ, whether we are in small groups, choirs, or congregations, bringing praise to God is a key element in our own expression of faith. And one day we'll be singing in a concert that defies imagination.

In a sweeping vision of the tumultuous events at the end of time, John records a chorus of praise that begins with a few saints and swells to a company beyond number. In honor of the Lamb of God, who with His blood has redeemed people from every tribe and nation (Revelation 5:9), the song begins at the throne of God, is joined by multiplied thousands of angels, and finally includes every creature in heaven, earth, and sea. Together we will sing, "To him who sits on the throne and to the Lamb be praise and honor and glory and power, for ever and ever!" (v. 13).

What a choir! What a concert! What a privilege to start rehearsing today!

—*David McCasland*

In *The Message* paraphrase, Revelation 19:1 reads like this: "I heard a sound like massed choirs in Heaven singing." It also says in Revelation 5: "I heard every creature in Heaven and earth, in underworld and sea, join in, all voices in all places, singing: To the One on the Throne! To the Lamb! The blessing, the honor, the glory, the strength, for age after age after age" (v. 13). There's lots of singing going on in heaven!

THE HYMN THAT BLESSED A QUEEN

Read: 1 Corinthians 10:1-4, 11

[They all] drank the same spiritual drink; for they drank from that spiritual rock that accompanied them, and that rock was Christ.
—1 CORINTHIANS 10:4

At the time of her golden jubilee in June 1887, Queen Victoria of the United Kingdom received dignitaries from all over the world. Among those who came to honor her was a representative from Madagascar. After conveying the good wishes of his people, he surprised Her Majesty by asking permission to sing for her. Those assembled thought he would choose one of his country's native songs, but they were amazed when he began, "Rock of Ages, cleft for me, let me hide myself in Thee." The rendition was so beautiful that it brought tears to the eyes of the Queen.

The author of that grand hymn, Augustus Toplady, was saved at the age of sixteen while attending a small evangelistic meeting in a rural district of Ireland. The sermon, preached by an illiterate layman, pointed Augustus to the Lord Jesus Christ—the Rock of Ages—in whom he could hide from God's wrath and find peace and forgiveness. As the young convert became established in his new faith, he felt God's call and began studying for the ministry. Since he was very frail, however, his fiery zeal and inspired efforts soon put too much strain on his weak body. Yet his faith never wavered. Augustus Toplady died of tuberculosis when he was only thirty-eight, but the lyrics he wrote—"Rock of Ages," firmly based on the Scriptures—still live on!

The next time you sing that old favorite, notice how the truths of salvation are expressed in all the verses. They will bless you as they did the Queen of England so many years ago.
—*Henry Bosch*

It has been noted by some that "Rock of Ages" was a favorite song of both Queen Victoria and of her husband, Prince Albert. According to author Robert D. Kalis, Prince Albert repeated the first stanza over and over while on his deathbed.

〤

WE'LL SING AND SHOUT!

Read: Revelation 21:1–5

Those who have leprosy are cleansed, the deaf hear.
—MATTHEW 11:5

I was enjoying a concert by a singing group when I noticed what was happening in the front rows of the auditorium. A sign-language interpreter was gracefully communicating the words of each song to about twenty-five people who were deaf.

When the vocalists sang "Victory in Jesus," the man who was both the pianist and emcee asked the translator if her group would "sing" the chorus. She agreed, and he began to play. No voices were heard, but we sat in awe as her group joyfully expressed the words with their hands. Their faces beamed, reflecting the meaning of each phrase.

I glanced at the five vocalists on the stage. Their faces were fixed intently on that group of twenty-five as they "sang" about victory in Jesus and praising our Savior forever. It was a thrilling experience.

I couldn't help but think of what it will be like in heaven. The hearing impaired will be able to hear and sing. They will be part of the vast chorus of the redeemed as they join the angels in proclaiming the praises of the Most High God and of the Lamb.

A day of rejoicing awaits every believer in Jesus Christ. We'll all be transformed, glorified, made whole. When we all get to heaven, we'll "sing and shout the victory."

—David Egner

———

The man who wrote "Victory in Jesus," Eugene Bartlett (1885-1941), was considered one of the key founders of the genre of Christian music called "Southern Gospel." He was inducted into the Gospel Music Hall of Fame in 1973. "Victory in Jesus" was the last of 800 songs Bartlett wrote in his life.

"GOD WILL TAKE CARE OF YOU"

Read: Psalm 34:9-17

Then they cried to the LORD in their trouble, and he saved them from their distress. —PSALM 107:13

In the early years of the twentieth century, Pastor W. Stillman Martin was scheduled to preach in a distant town, yet he was worried about leaving home because his wife had become ill. After pondering and praying about his problem, he mentioned it to his children. One of them gave the advice he needed. "Don't be afraid to go, Father. I'm sure God will take good care of Mother while you're away." The pastor remembered how he had often impressed upon them that they should put the Lord first in their lives. So he went in the confidence of Psalm 37:23, believing that the Lord was ordering his steps.

The services were richly blessed by God; and when he returned home, his wife was much improved. In gratitude to the Lord, Civilla Martin wrote a poem about God's loving help and providential care. Within an hour, her husband had improvised a melody on the organ to fit the words. It has become a famous and much-loved hymn:

Be not dismayed whate'er betide, God will take care of you;
Beneath His wings of love abide, God will take care of you.

Troubled believer, the Lord is interested in you and your problems. Call upon Him, and He will take care of you.

—*Henry Bosch*

———

One person who was helped by Stillman and Civilla Martin's song was entrepreneur J. C. Penney. While recuperating from financially hard times, Penney entered a sanitarium where he heard the song. This prompted him to visit the chapel on the grounds and turn his life back to God.

LIGHTS ON?

Read: Matthew 5:13-16

For you were once darkness, but now you are light in the Lord.
Live as children of light. —EPHESIANS 5:8

On a dark and stormy night with waves piling up like mountains on Lake Erie, a ship rocked and plunged near the Cleveland harbor. "Are we on course?" asked the captain, seeing only one beacon from the lighthouse. "Quite sure, sir," replied the officer at the helm. "Where are the lower lights?" "Gone out, sir." "Can we make the harbor?" "We must, or perish!" came the reply. With a steady hand and a stalwart heart, the officer headed the ship toward land. But in the darkness he missed the channel and the vessel was dashed to pieces on the rocks. Many lives were lost in a watery grave. This incident moved Philip P. Bliss to write the familiar hymn, "Let the Lower Lights Be Burning."

Jesus, the Light of the world, has gone to heaven. Now Christians have the responsibility to be the "lower lights" that guide sinners to the harbor of His redeeming grace.

How can we be sure that we are reflecting God's love to others? By voicing David's prayer, "Search me, God, and know my heart; test me and know my anxious thoughts. See if there is any offensive way in me, and lead me in the way everlasting" (Psalm 139:23–24). If we forsake every sin that then comes to mind, we can be certain our light is shining brightly in a dark and needy world.

—Dennis DeHaan

The story about the Lake Erie shipwreck that prompted this song came from a message by D. L. Moody, with whom Bliss was sometimes associated as a singer or song leader. After Bliss heard the story, he wrote about the believer's responsibility to keep the "lower lights" burning to guide others to the safety of the Savior.

DON'T FORGET TO CROWN HIM!

Read: Romans 14:7-11

"Why do you call me 'Lord, Lord,' and do not do what I say?"
—LUKE 6:46

Christ wants to be crowned king of our lives. Some of God's children are content to let Him save their souls but refuse to submit their bodies to Him as a living sacrifice (Romans 12:1–2).

A heartwarming story in the book *Forward Day by Day* tells about a song that especially delights youngsters. It's called "Praise Him, All Ye Little Children." Sitting at the piano one day, a father and his young boy were singing it together. It is one of those gospel hymns that runs on and on with many satisfying but seemingly endless verses. They sang several stanzas:

> *Praise Him, praise Him, all ye little children,*
> *God is love, God is love . . .*
> *Love Him, love Him, all ye little children . . .*
> *Thank Him, thank Him, all ye little children . . .*
> *Serve Him, serve Him, all ye little children.*

Then the father stopped. The boy looked up in surprise, still expecting more. "Dad, you forgot to crown Him!" he said. And so once again they lifted their voices and sang, "Crown Him, crown Him, all ye little children." Without realizing it, the child had emphasized a great biblical truth. As believers we say we love Christ and may even serve Him, but often we fail to give Him absolute control. Instead, we insist on governing our lives, and we refuse to yield completely to Him.

Jesus deserves your best, for He has bought you, soul and body. Don't forget to crown Him Lord of all!

—*Henry Bosch*

Nobody knows who wrote the lyrics for "Praise Him, All Ye Little Children," but Carey Bonner wrote the music.

"IN THE SWEET BY AND BY"

Read: Romans 8:18-28

I consider that our present sufferings are not worth comparing with the glory that will be revealed in us. —ROMANS 8:18

The gifted Christian musician Joseph P. Webster (1819–1875) was often tormented by deep feelings of depression. On one occasion when he was in a melancholy mood, he received a visit from his close acquaintance Sanford Fillmore Bennett. Knowing that one way to keep Webster from brooding over his problems was to interest him in writing a hymn tune, Bennett decided he'd try to pen some lyrics that would direct his friend's thoughts heavenward.

The despondent man himself unwittingly supplied the theme, for when he was asked, "What's the matter now?" he replied, "Oh, it will be all right by and by!" "That's true," exclaimed Bennett, "trials do generate great glory for us in the sweet by and by!" Inspired by this thought, he immediately sat down and wrote several poetic verses on the subject. When his friend read them, a new look of hope came into his eyes, and his whole attitude changed. After jotting down some musical notes, Webster took up his violin and played the melody he had composed to fit the words. The enduring hymn "In the Sweet By and By" was born.

It helped the musician see his trials in the light of heaven, for the lyrics read in part:

There's a land that is fairer than day, and by faith we can see it afar,
For the Father waits over the way to prepare us a dwelling-place there.
We shall sing on that beautiful shore the melodious songs of the blest;
And our spirits shall sorrow no more—not a sigh for the blessing of rest.

Yes, heaven's rewards will far outweigh earth's tears "in the sweet by and by."

—*Henry Bosch*

According to Bennett, it took no more than thirty minutes for Bennett and Joseph Webster to write both the words and music for "In the Sweet By and By." Bennett jotted the words down and turned them over
to Webster, who quickly wrote the music.

〤

THE MAKING OF US

Read: Romans 8:18-29

For those God foreknew he also predestined to be conformed to the image of his Son, that he might be the firstborn among many brothers and sisters.
—ROMANS 8:29

In a book by Robert V. Ozment entitled *But God Can*, some interesting observations are quoted from the Scottish author George MacDonald. Telling of a woman who had encountered a great tragedy in her life, he says, "The heartache was so crushing and her sorrow so bitter that the one in distress exclaimed, 'I wish I'd never been made.' With spiritual discernment, her friend answered, 'My dear, you are not fully made yet, you're only being made, and this is the Maker's process!' " MacDonald wisely concludes, "We can let God take our troubles and make out of them a garment of Christian fortitude that will not only warm our souls but also serve to inspire others."

Apparent tragedies became the making of some men. Milton, despite the blindness which overtook him, wrote the incomparable *Paradise Lost*. Beethoven became deaf but nevertheless wrote mighty music that made him famous. George Matheson went blind at college, but his majestic hymn "O Love That Wilt Not Let Me Go" is universally sung throughout the world.

Does it seem as though everything in life is going against you? Have friends forsaken you, and are your dreams and aspirations shattered? As you face these disillusionments, take heart! If you're a child of God, you may be sure that all things are working "for good." Rightly received, these experiences can truly be the making of you.

—*Richard DeHaan*

George Matheson wrote "O Love . . ." in five minutes on the evening his sister was married. Apparently, her marriage reminded him of being rejected by his fiancée when he had gone blind some twenty years earlier. In his sadness, he wrote this song.

THE BLIND CARVER'S HYMN

Read: Psalm 55:1-6, 16-17

Lord, they came to you in their distress; when you disciplined them, they could barely whisper a prayer. —ISAIAH 26:16

Everyone in Coleshill, England, knew Bill Walford. During the week, he was forever whittling novelties for the children, and he managed to make a scant living by carving keepsake items and selling them in a little shop.

Having experienced many "seasons of distress and grief," he had come to rely upon the Lord, finding relief from his troubles as he pondered the promises of the Word and prayed. He was only a layman but was often asked to preach in different churches by the spiritual leaders in his community who were all his friends. Although his life was filled with adversity, there was something uplifting about the elderly man's outlook on life.

One day in 1842 a minister named Thomas Salmon stopped in Walford's shop. Walford had a poem on prayer running through his mind and asked Brother Salmon to take down the words as he recited them before they slipped from his memory. While he had rare spiritual insight, the reason Walford asked for help was that physically he was totally blind! Years later a copy of that verse came to the attention of New York organist and composer William Bradbury. He immediately saw in Walford's poem the material for a comforting hymn, and in a short time wrote the tune.

You can live again that blind carver's spiritual emotions if you pay close attention to the words the next time you sing "Sweet Hour of Prayer."

—*Henry Bosch*

One of the things Bill Walford did with his mind was to memorize large portions of Scripture. Some people in his community thought he might have memorized the entire Bible. "Sweet Hour of Prayer" was Walford's only verse ever put to music.

GOD'S UNCHANGING WORD

Read: 1 Peter 1:15-25

Your word, LORD, is eternal; it stands firm in the heavens.
—PSALM 119:89

Henry Francis Lyte (1793–1847), the author of the well-known hymn "Abide with Me," lived long ago, but his lyrics ring true today. Listen to his words:

> *Swift to its close ebbs out life's little day;*
> *Earth's joys grow dim, its glories pass away;*
> *Change and decay in all around I see—*
> *O Thou who changest not, abide with me.*

We live in an atmosphere of change. Today more than ever before, it appears that almost everything is in a state of flux. Very little seems to endure. Many well-established foundations are being shaken. The world is "on the move." As a result, this generation is restless, insecure, and uncertain of who they are, why they are here, and where they are going. In such a day we should be thankful that there are some things that abide. First of all, we know a Person who never changes—One in whom we can place our trust and believe with all our hearts. We serve a God who is the same yesterday, today, and forever. He said, "I the LORD do not change" (Malachi 3:6). There are also absolutes, principles, and abiding truths to guide and comfort us. These can be found in the Bible, the Word of God.

The psalmist declared, "Your word, LORD, is eternal; it stands firm in the heavens" (Psalm 119:89). Given to us by an immutable God, the Scriptures are His eternal truth. It is the message that groping, lost souls need today. Thank God for the Bible—His unchanging Word in a changing world!

—*Richard DeHaan*

The writer of "Abide with Me," Henry Lyte, died from tuberculosis three weeks after penning this song.

"ABIDE WITH ME" . . .
AND SOCCER?

Read: Hebrews 13:1-8

Keep your lives free from the love of money and be content with what
you have, because God has said, "Never will I leave you;
never will I forsake you." —HEBREWS 13:5

One of the highlights of English football (soccer) each year is the final match of the annual FA Cup Final. For more than a hundred years, the day has been marked by excitement, festivity, and competition. But what fascinates me is how the game begins. It starts with the singing of Henry Lyte's traditional hymn "Abide with Me."

At first that struck me as odd. What does that hymn have to do with football? As I thought about it, though, I realized that for the follower of Christ it has everything to do with sports, shopping, working, going to school, or anything else we do. Since there is no corner of our lives that should not be affected by the presence of God, the longing that He would abide with us is actually the most reasonable thing we could desire. Of course, the presence of our heavenly Father is not something we need to plead for—it is promised to us. In Hebrews 13:5, we read, "God has said, 'Never will I leave you; never will I forsake you.' "

Not only is God's presence the key to our contentment, but it is also the promise that can give us wisdom, peace, comfort, and strength—no matter where we are or what we are doing.

—*Bill Crowder*

One of the most stirring renditions of "Abide with Me" in an English football venue is one by Hayley Westenra of New Zealand as she leads the crowd in this time-honored song.

HEART MUSIC

Read: Psalm 98

Let the message of Christ dwell among you richly as you teach and admonish one another with all wisdom through psalms, hymns, and songs from the Spirit, singing to God with gratitude in your hearts.
—COLOSSIANS 3:16

We are encouraged in the Scriptures to sing. Whether songs of praise, worship, adoration, or dedication, they should emanate from the heart.

Some good questions to ask yourself before the next song service begins at church are these: Do I really mean what I'm singing? Is this coming from my heart, or am I just going through the motions?

We sing "'Tis the Blessed Hour of Prayer" and then allow our thoughts to wander aimlessly while we or others pray. We plead with enthusiasm, "Bring Them In" and later gripe about the repeated call for people to do outreach. We sing "For the Beauty of the Earth" and then pollute it with garbage and debris. We raise our voices to ask, "Is It the Crowning Day?" and proceed to live as though we had never heard of the Savior's return. We love the hymn "Holy Bible, Book Divine" but spend most of our time reading novels and poring over websites. We declare in song, "I Love to Tell the Story" and can't remember the last time we spoke a word for Christ. We sing "Just One Step at a Time" and immediately begin to worry about tomorrow!

This is not singing from our hearts. Someone has observed that "when the heart moves devoutly with the voice, true heart-singing results." I would add that it is whenever "the heart and hand move devoutly with the voice." The sincerity of our devotion is demonstrated by what we sing and do. When our songs are matched by our deeds—this is heart music!

—*Richard DeHaan*

Folliott S. Pierpoint (1835–1917), who wrote the song "For the Beauty of the Earth," was overwhelmed by the natural magnificence of his region in England near the town of Bath. The region's limestone hills have been labeled an Area of Outstanding Natural Beauty.

◊

WHEREFORE, STAND!

Read: Ephesians 6:10-18

Put on the full armor of God, so that you can take your stand against the devil's schemes. —EPHESIANS 6:11

In the year 1858 a great revival occurred in the city of Philadelphia. The godly evangelist was Dudley A. Tyng. At one meeting during the campaign, the crowd swelled to over 5,000 people. Pastor Tyng chose as his text Exodus 10:11, which reads, "Go now ye that are men, and serve the LORD" (KJV). And during the message, he said he would rather lose his right arm than stop proclaiming God's Word. It was a soul-stirring sermon.

A few days later, Tyng entered a barn where a mule was providing the power for a corn-shelling machine. The evangelist patted the animal on the neck with one hand, but the sleeve on his other arm got caught in the mechanism. The arm was badly mangled, and in a few hours Tyng died from loss of blood. Just before his death, however, he sent a message to the men who had been his associates in the revival work. "Tell them," he said, "to stand up for Jesus!" On the following Sunday, George Duffield preached at his own church taking for his text Ephesians 6:14: "Stand firm then, with the belt of truth buckled around your waist, with the breastplate of righteousness in place." At the close of the message, he read a poem he had written embodying the dying words and sentiments of his departed friend Dudley Tyng. It was later set to a stirring tune and became the well-known hymn "Stand Up for Jesus."

One of the best ways for each of us to give glory and honor to our God is to "Stand up for Jesus."

—*Henry Bosch*

After hearing Rev. George Duffield read his new poem, his Sunday school superintendent, Benedict Stewart, had a number of copies printed. Soon the song appeared in *The Sabbath Hymn Book*, and it later became a favorite of Civil War soldiers.

HE IS HERE!

Read: Psalm 145:13-21

The LORD is near to all who call on him. —PSALM 145:18

God's promise to be with His people (Psalm 145:18) is a wonderful gift that we sometimes take for granted. But there are times in every believer's life when His presence becomes a precious reality.

A few years ago I sank into an uncharacteristic period of anxiety and depression. After many years of spiritual and emotional stability, I was nearly overwhelmed with dark thoughts. I struggled to counteract the despair with the truths of God and the help of the Holy Spirit.

Then one night I went to a gospel concert. During the concert, I heard a song I was not familiar with. I listened as the group sang a song entitled "He Is Here."

The song expressed one of the most familiar truths of the Bible—a truth I had long taken for granted—our God is with us. But how it spoke to me that night! It brought me unbelievable comfort, release, and hope. The Lord used that gospel song to spark a turnaround in my life. I began to appreciate God's presence in a fresh and invigorating way.

As God's children, we may think we should be exempt from emotional struggles. But we aren't.

If it seems as if God has left you, if you are despondent, if you feel alone and afraid, meditate on the truth of the song title "He Is Here."

—David Egner

The song "He Is Here" was named the 1992 Dove Award Song of the Year, and it received a nomination for a Grammy Award.

JONAH ON BOARD

Read: Jonah 1-2

This terrified them and they asked, "What have you done?" (They knew he was running away from the LORD, because he had already told them so.)
—JONAH 1:10

The year is 1748. A trading ship departs from an island off the west coast of Africa headed for England. Aboard is John Newton, a seaman with a reputation for profane language and ungodly living. As Newton later described it, the captain "would often tell me that to his grief he had a Jonah on board; that a curse attended me wherever I went, and that all the troubles he met with in the voyage were owing to his having taken me into the vessel."

The captain may have been right. Newton had earlier turned his back on God. But just as a storm had threatened to destroy the boat bearing Jonah, so too a fierce Atlantic wind rudely awakened John Newton. The vessel nearly broke apart. As the damaged ship drifted at sea, Newton prayed for God's mercy and put his faith in Jesus. That's how a blasphemous, disreputable seaman became, by God's grace, the godly penman of the words of the beloved hymn "Amazing Grace."

If you, like Jonah, are a child of God who has strayed or who has deliberately run away from the Lord, come home. Live for Him again. Or maybe you're like John Newton. You need to trust Jesus for salvation. Don't wait for one of life's storms to awaken you to your need. Turn to Christ today.

—*Dave Branon*

After he became a pastor, John Newton spoke to a congregation that included William Wilberforce and had some amount of influence on him. Wilberforce was a key figure in the move to abolish slavery in the nineteenth century in England.

TRULY AMAZING GRACE!

Read: Ephesians 2:1-10

By grace you have been saved, through faith. —EPHESIANS 2:8

But by the grace of God I am what I am. —1 CORINTHIANS 15:10

When Paul told the believers at Ephesus that salvation was by grace and not by works, he knew what he was talking about. If anyone had reason to boast of his religious accomplishments, Paul did. But he recognized how worthless his deeds were, and he knew that his religious zeal had actually blinded him to the plan and purpose of God. His persecution of the early church had put many believers in prison. Yet the Lord called this man to be His "chosen vessel" to take the gospel to the Gentiles. The grace of God had turned a murderer into a missionary.

A friend called on John Newton, author of the beloved hymn "Amazing Grace," in the later years of his life. A portion of Scripture was read, including the verse, "By the grace of God I am what I am" (1 Corinthians 15:10). Newton then commented, "I am not what I ought to be. How imperfect and deficient! I am not what I wish to be. I abhor what is evil, and I would cleave to what is good. I am not what I hope to be. Soon I shall put off mortality, all sin, and imperfection. Yet though I am not what I ought to be, nor what I wish to be, nor what I hope to be, I can truly say I am not what I once was—a slave to sin and Satan. I can heartily join with the apostle and acknowledge, 'By the grace of God I am what I am.' "

If you have been saved through faith in Jesus' sacrifice on the cross, you can say that too. Thank God for His amazing grace!

—Richard DeHaan

Among the influential Christians Newton befriended after he had become a Christian and given up slave trading were preachers George Whitfield and John Wesley and poet William Cowper.

HOLD THE FORT

Read: Revelation 2:25-29

Hold on to what you have until I come. —REVELATION 2:25

One of the favorite hymns of my father, Dr. M. R. DeHaan, was "Hold the Fort." Deeply aware of the spiritual battle in which we as believers are engaged, and eagerly looking for the coming of the Lord, how he loved to sing:

My comrades, see the signal waving in the sky!
Reinforcements now appearing, victory is nigh.
See the mighty hosts advancing,
Satan leading on; mighty men around us falling, courage almost gone!
"Hold the fort, for I am coming," Jesus signals still.
Wave the answer back to heaven, "By Thy grace we will."

In his book *Moody's Anecdotes*, J. B. McClure related this story: "When General Sherman went through Atlanta toward the sea in the Civil War, he left in the fort, back in the Kennesaw Mountains, a little handful of men to guard some rations. Confederate General Hood, however, attacked the fort, and the battle raged furiously. Half the defenders were either killed or badly hurt, and the general in command was wounded seven different times. When they were just about ready to surrender, Sherman got within 15 miles of the besieged camp, and, through the signal corps on a nearby mountain, sent the message: 'Hold fast; we are coming. W. T. Sherman.' That message fired up the beleaguered troops, and they held out till reinforcements came. They kept the fort from the hands of the enemy. Sherman said while he did not actually say the words 'hold the fort,' that was his intent."

Our heavenly commander has given us the same challenge. The last promise in the Bible is from the lips of the Lord Jesus who said, "Yes, I am coming soon" (Revelation 22:20). So, with patience, courage, and hope, let us endure until the victory is won.

—*Richard DeHaan*

Philip P. Bliss, who wrote the song "Hold the Fort," heard this story about General Sherman in 1870 during a Sunday school class when someone retold the tale.

HOW CAN WE KEEP FROM SINGING?

From God's Hymnbook: Psalm 146

I will praise the LORD all my life; I will sing praise to my God as long as I live. —PSALM 146:2

Robert Lowry (1826–1899) felt that preaching would be his greatest contribution in life. However, this pastor is best remembered for his music. Lowry composed words or music for more than 500 songs, including "Christ Arose," "I Need Thee Every Hour," and "Shall We Gather at the River?"

In 1860, as the United States teetered on the brink of civil war, Lowry wrote these enduring words that focus not on threatening circumstances but on the unchanging Christ:

> *What though my joys and comforts die?*
> *The Lord my Savior liveth;*
> *What though the darkness gather round!*
> *Songs in the night He giveth:*
> *No storm can shake my inmost calm*
> *While to that refuge clinging;*
> *Since Christ is Lord of Heav'n and earth,*
> *How can I keep from singing?*

Lowry's confidence in God during difficult times echoes the psalmist's words: "Do not put your trust in princes, in human beings, who cannot save. . . . Blessed are those whose help is the God of Jacob, whose hope is in the LORD their God" (Psalm 146:3–5).

Whether we react to life with faith or fear depends on our focus. Knowing that "the LORD reigns forever" (v. 10), how can we keep from singing?

—David McCasland

Robert Lowry wrote "We're Marching to Zion," "Nothing but the Blood," "Oh, Worship the Lord," and many other favorites.

THE LOVE OF GOD

Read: Ephesians 3:18-19

To know this love that surpasses knowledge. —EPHESIANS 3:19

The lyrics of the hymn "The Love of God" by Frederick Lehman (1868–1953) capture in word pictures the breathtaking magnitude of divine love:

> *Could we with ink the ocean fill*
> *And were the skies of parchment made,*
> *Were every stalk on earth a quill,*
> *And every man a scribe by trade,*
> *To write the love of God above*
> *Would drain the ocean dry,*
> *Nor could the scroll contain the whole*
> *Though stretched from sky to sky.*

These marvelous lyrics echo Paul's response to the love of God. The apostle prayed that believers might "have power, together with all the Lord's holy people, to grasp how wide and long and high and deep is the love of Christ, and to know this love that surpasses knowledge" (Ephesians 3:18–19). In reflecting on these verses about God's love, some Bible scholars believe "width" refers to its worldwide embrace (John 3:16); "length," its existence through all ages (Ephesians 3:21); "depth," its profound wisdom (Romans 11:33); and "height," its victory over sin opening the way to heaven (Ephesians 4:8).

As we expand our awareness of God's love, we soon realize that its full measure is beyond our understanding. Even if the ocean itself were filled with ink, using it to write about the love of God would drain it dry.

—Dennis Fisher

———

Frederick Lehman wrote this song in 1917 while working for a fruit-packing company in California putting oranges and lemons in crates. Some of the lyrics for the song were added later.

GAINING FROM LOSING

Read: Psalm 143

Let the morning bring me word of your unfailing love, for I have put my trust in you. Show me the way I should go, for to you I entrust my life.
—PSALM 143:8

The great composer Ludwig van Beethoven (1770–1827) lived much of his life in fear of deafness. He was concerned because he felt the sense of hearing was essential to creating music of lasting value.

When Beethoven discovered that the thing he feared most was coming rapidly upon him, he was almost frantic with anxiety. He consulted doctors and tried every possible remedy. But the deafness increased until at last all hearing was gone.

Beethoven finally found the strength he needed to go on despite his great loss. To everyone's amazement, he wrote some of his grandest music after he became totally deaf. With all distractions shut out, melodies flooded in on him as fast as his pen could write them down. His deafness became a great asset.

Many Christians can testify of the deeper joys experienced when a great loss isolated them from the world around them. It was then that they cried out to the Lord and could hear for the first time the voice of God reassuring them of His unfailing love and grace. It put a song of praise in their hearts.

Child of God, have you experienced a great loss? Don't lose hope. Call on the Lord. Trust Him and keep listening. If you do, you will gain even from loss.

—*Henry Bosch*

Beethoven's marvelous music from his Ninth Symphony was used to accompany the words of Henry van Dyke's amazing poem "Joyful, Joyful, We Adore Thee." Beethoven's Ninth was written by the composer in the 1820s; van Dyke wrote the words in 1907.

ARE YOU AFRAID?

Read: Psalm 56

When I am afraid, I will put my trust in you. —PSALM 56:3

Hotly pursued by his enemies the Philistines, the psalmist David was understandably afraid. Who wouldn't be! In many circumstances fear is natural. God made us with that capacity. But this powerful emotion, unless controlled, can either stop us dead in our tracks or make us run like a scared rabbit.

David countered this paralysis/panic reaction by putting his faith in God and praising His Word. One Bible translation renders Psalm 56:4 this way: "In God, whose word I praise— in God I trust and am not afraid."

Christians can find the same help today when gripped by fear of an enemy. Captain Dundy Aipoalani was an F-16 pilot during Operation Desert Storm. He wrote, "I was scared many times during my twenty-eight missions over Iraq and Kuwait, but I hung on to the cross of Jesus and trusted in His love. Sometimes on my missions I would get so nervous that I would sing, 'Jesus loves me, this I know, for the Bible tells me so.' " It was all he could remember, but it was enough to know that Jesus loved him. God said so.

Afraid? Trust God and remind yourself of His love for you in Christ. Fear may not suddenly evaporate, but trusting God and praising His Word will prevent panic and strengthen you to go on.

—*Dennis DeHaan*

The popular little song "Jesus Loves Me, This I Know" was written in 1860 by a woman named Anna Bartlett Warner (she also wrote "We Would See Jesus"). The music was added a few years later by William Bradbury. An eclectic group of entertainers have record- ed this song: Ray Stevens, Whitney Houston, Rosemary Clooney, the group Alabama, and Dionne Warwick.

WORSHIP HIS MAJESTY

Read: Revelation 19:11–16

On his robe and on his thigh he has this name written: KING OF KINGS AND LORD OF LORDS. —REVELATION 19:16

Jack Hayford and his wife, Anna, were vacationing in Great Britain during the 25th anniversary of the coronation of Queen Elizabeth II in 1978. While there, the Hayfords saw constant reminders of royalty. That, along with visits to several castles, caused Hayford to sense what it might be like to be "raised as a child in such regal settings." With this in mind, he asked Anna to write down some lyrics one day as they drove through the countryside: Those words spoke of God's majesty, emphasizing the power and praise that goes to Jesus. Thus the glorious praise song "Majesty" was born.

In Scripture, Jesus is called "High Priest," "Prince of Peace," "Lamb of God," Bread of Life," "Light of the World," "Good Shepherd." But perhaps the most magnificent, awe-inspiring title is "King of Kings." It reminds us that His power far surpasses that of any mortal ruler. It suggests to us the splendor of the ultimate kingdom in which He will reign forever. What's most amazing is that we who know Christ as Savior are children of the King.

How should we respond? Hayford's song suggests that each day we should lift in praise Jesus' name as we give Him glory. Yes, our primary task in life is to worship His Majesty.

—*Dave Branon*

In a survey conducted by *Christianity Today* magazine, Jack Hayford's song "Majesty" was voted as one of the ten best worship songs of all time.

HEAVEN WITHOUT JESUS?

Read: Revelation 22:1-5

They will see his face, and his name will be on their foreheads.
—REVELATION 22:4

When John W. Peterson (1921–2006) first started writing gospel melodies and lyrics, some were rejected by publishers. One such occurrence was especially disturbing to the young musician. Peterson had just written "Over the Sunset Mountains" after meditating on that glorious day when we will enter the joys of heaven and see the Savior. The music editor he approached seemed pleased with his song but made this small suggestion: "Take out the name Jesus, and enlarge a little more on heaven." Peterson thought, *Heaven without Jesus? That is unthinkable!* So he picked up his manuscript and left.

Soon another song came into his mind that expressed his heartfelt reaction:

> *I have no song to sing, but that of Christ my King;*
> *To Him my praise I'll bring forevermore!*
> *His love beyond degree, His death that ransomed me;*
> *Now and eternally, I'll sing it o'er.[1]*

God honored John Peterson for not compromising the truth. Eventually both songs were published, and over the years they have brought comfort to many.

As a Christian, Peterson couldn't think of heaven without Christ. He knew that when believers are facing death, they are comforted in the knowledge that joy awaits them in the presence of their Lord.

—*Henry Bosch*

During John W. Peterson's prodigious career in music, he wrote more than a thousand songs and thirty-five cantatas.

1. "My Song" © 1954 John W. Peterson Music Company. All rights reserved. Used by permission.

"BRING US LIGHT"

Read: Luke 1:67-69

Because of the tender mercy of our God, by which the rising sun will come to us from heaven to shine on those living in darkness and in the shadow of death, to guide our feet into the path of peace. —LUKE 1:78–79

As hard as she tried, Joni Eareckson could not get into the Christmas spirit. It was Christmas Eve, and she was seated in church with her friends. Candles lined the sanctuary. Boughs of green pine decked with red ribbon were everywhere. A soft snow swirled outside. Everything was perfect—except Joni.

As the congregation sang, she did not feel a single stirring of adoration or praise. "It's no use," her heart cried. "I'm a failure." So she sulked. Then the bittersweet, wistful strains of a familiar carol reached her heart. From "O Come, O Come, Emmanuel" came the words, "And ransom captive Israel, that mourns in lonely exile here." This described her feelings.

The song continued, "O come, Thou Dayspring, come and cheer our spirits by Thine advent here; O drive away the shades of night and pierce the clouds and bring us light." "That's how I feel!" she cried out in her soul. She bowed and asked the Lord to take the gloom away and bring her cheer—and He did!

What happened to Joni happens to all who respond in faith to Jesus—whether they are receiving Him as their Savior or are renewing fellowship with Him. He came to drive away the darkness of guilt and gloom and replace it with the light of His joy and peace. O come, Immanuel!

—*David Egner*

Unlike most of the songs we sing today, "O Come, O Come, Emmanuel" does not have a known author. The lyrics were apparently passed down through the centuries from the twelfth century and translated from Latin to English. The tune has been credited to songwriter Thomas Helmore in the mid-1800s.

PEOPLE WHO SING!

Read: Psalm 96

[They] sang the song of God's servant Moses and of the Lamb: "Great and marvelous are your deeds, Lord God Almighty. Just and true are your ways, King of the nations." —REVELATION 15:3

Emperor penguins love to sing. They are among the most musical creatures on earth. When courting, the male and female bow and sing to each other. Her voice is soft and gentle; he sings loud and long. When the mother penguin has laid her eggs, she goes off to the ocean for several weeks to feed. While she is gone, the father sits on the eggs and sings. After regaining her strength, the female comes back to the nest and sings as well. And shortly before a little one is hatched, if you lean your ear down close to the shell, you can hear the chick singing inside.

The people of God are also singers. When Moses led Israel out of Egypt, he paused to praise God in song (Exodus 15:1–18). Deborah sang in victory (Judges 5). David's songs were numerous. Many psalms begin with a reference to singing (66, 81, 89, 92, 95, 96, 98, 101, 138, 149). The disciples sang in the upper room (Mark 14:26). Paul instructed believers to sing (Ephesians 5:19; Colossians 3:16). And our verse for today tells of the song of the redeemed in heaven.

Are we singing Christians? Are we expressing the joy of the Lord in song? It may not always be on our lips, but it should resound in our hearts and minds. If you have no song, something is wrong. Christians are a people who can't help but sing!

—*David Egner*

The biblical book of the Psalms is the part of the Bible that is most often set to music, which makes sense because some of the psalms were songs in the day in which they were penned (Songs of Ascent, for instance, in Psalms 120-134). There have been projects in which musicians have turned all 150 psalms into songs.

SPACE MUSIC

Read: Job 38:1-7

On what were [the earth's] footings set, or who laid its cornerstone—while the morning stars sang together and all the angels shouted for joy?
—JOB 38:6–7

One of NASA's observatories has discovered a giant black hole that hums. Located in the Perseus cluster of galaxies about 250 million light years from Earth, the black hole vibrates at the frequency of a B flat. But it is too low a pitch to be picked up by the human ear. Scientific instruments have placed the note at 57 octaves below middle C on a piano.

The idea of music and heavenly bodies is not new. In fact, when God revealed himself to Job, He asked: "Where were you when I laid the earth's foundation? . . . While the morning stars sang together and all the angels shouted for joy?" (Job 38:4, 7). We are told that at the creation of our marvelous universe, songs of praise and shouts of joy resounded to God's glory.

A wonderful hymn by St. Francis of Assisi captures the awe and worship we feel when beholding the radiant sun by day or the star-studded sky at night.

All creatures of our God and King,
Lift up your voice and with us sing Alleluia, Alleluia!
Thou burning sun with golden beam,
Thou silver moon with softer gleam:
O praise Him, O praise Him! Alleluia! Alleluia! Alleluia!

Let's praise the One who made such beauty for us to enjoy!
—*Dennis Fisher*

St. Francis lived from 1182 to 1226 in Italy, and this song was written near the end of his life. He apparently wrote more than fifty songs for the men who lived in the monastery where he served. It has been said that he requested Psalm 140 to be read as he lay dying in October 1226.

STRUGGLES AND SONGS

Read: Psalm 13

My heart rejoices in your salvation. —PSALM 13:5

William Cowper (pronounced "Cooper"), an eighteenth-century English poet and hymn writer (1731–1800), struggled with recurring bouts of depression throughout his life. Perhaps that's why his hymns still touch us deeply during times when our life seems to be spinning out of control and we desperately want to trust God.

One of Cowper's best-known hymns, "God Moves in a Mysterious Way," contains these encouraging words:

> *Ye fearful saints, fresh courage take;*
> *The clouds ye so much dread*
> *Are big with mercy and shall break*
> *In blessings on your head.*

We often imagine that the triumphal songs of faith were penned by people who had already overcome their struggles. But the Bible's songbook—the Psalms—reminds us that the anguished cries of "How long, LORD? Will you forget me forever? How long will you hide your face from me?" sometimes occur in almost the same breath as "My heart rejoices in your salvation. I will sing the LORD's praise, for he has been good to me" (Psalm 13:1, 5–6).

In every struggle—mental, physical, emotional, or spiritual—our challenge is to move from the fear of being overwhelmed to the confidence that God has overcome. Cowper didn't find it easy, but he always found that God was greater than he had ever imagined.

Facing clouds today? Take courage! Your greatest praise to God may be sung in the darkest days of your life.

—*David McCasland*

William Cowper was a close friend of John Newton, and they collaborated on a songbook called *Olney Hymns*, published in 1779. Cowper also wrote "There Is a Fountain Filled with Blood."

⋊⋉

REST INTO IT

Read: Romans 8:31-39

"Come to me, all you who are weary and burdened, and I will give you rest." —MATTHEW 11:28

The most enjoyable part of the stretch-and-flex exercise class I attend is the last five minutes. That's when we lie flat on our backs on our mats with the lights down low for relaxation. During one of those times, our instructor said softly, "Find a place where you can rest into." I thought of the best place to "rest into" mentioned in the words of a hymn by Cleland B. McAfee, "Near to the Heart of God."

There is a place of quiet rest, near to the heart of God,
A place where sin cannot molest, near to the heart of God.
O Jesus, blest Redeemer, sent from the heart of God,
Hold us who wait before Thee near to the heart of God.

This hymn was written in 1903 after the death of McAfee's two nieces from diphtheria. His church choir sang it outside the quarantine home of his brother, offering words of hope about God's heart of care.

The apostle Paul tells us that God has a heart of love for us (Romans 8:31–39). Nothing—not tribulation, distress, persecution, famine, nakedness, peril, sword, death, life, angels, principalities, powers, height, nor depth—is able to separate us from the enduring love of our Lord. "If God is for us, who can be against us?" (v. 31).

Whatever our stresses or concerns, the heart of God is the place to "rest into." Leave it all with Him, "because he cares for you" (1 Peter 5:7).

—Anne Cetas

Cleland McAfee (1866-1944) pastored churches in Chicago and Brooklyn during his career. He also spent many years as a seminary professor.

MOZART'S PET BIRD

Read: Psalm 104:1–13

The birds of the sky nest by the waters; they sing among the branches.
—PSALM 104:12

Wolfgang Amadeus Mozart (1756–1791) is revered as a genius of musical composition. In one instance, he was even inspired by the melody of a bird. Mozart had a pet starling whose song so fascinated him that some say he wrote a piece of music based on the melody he heard in the bird's chirps.

Birds were also an inspiration to the psalmist. In Psalm 104, he praises God for caring for the living creatures He put on the earth. Included in his observations are birds who fly in the heavens above, perch in the branches of trees, and sing songs of heartfelt joy: "The birds of the sky nest by the waters; they sing among the branches" (v. 12). Nature filled the psalmist's heart with praise to God, and I think that must have included the musical sounds of the birds.

Often the marvels we see in creation prompt us to worship. This theme is repeated throughout Scripture: "The heavens declare the glory of God; the skies proclaim the work of his hands" (Psalm 19:1). Creation's stimulus to praise need not be limited to the visual. It can also be widened to include hearing nature's songs. As we go about our daily routine, we can tune our hearts to the melodies God has placed in His creatures and let them serve as an added springboard of praise to the Creator.

—*Dennis Fisher*

———

Mozart bought his pet starling on May 27, 1784, for thirty-four kreutzer (a German coin). The bird lived at the Mozart home until it died three years later. Like many of us have who have lost a pet, Mozart buried the deceased songbird in the backyard.

MEETING AT THE FOUNTAIN

Read: Revelation 7:9-17

The Lamb at the center of the throne will be their shepherd; he will lead them to springs of living water. —REVELATION 7:17

One of the outstanding composers of gospel hymns in the nineteenth century was Philip P. Bliss. Saved at an early age, he wrote such songs as "Hold the Fort," "Wonderful Words of Life," "Hallelujah, 'Tis Done," and "Almost Persuaded."

The story about the writing of one of his compositions is not too well known. When Bliss joined evangelist D. L. Moody in Chicago, a great industrial exposition was being held. One of its central attractions was a grand fountain. It became the place where people frequently gathered. One would say to another, "Will you meet me at the fountain?" Bliss was struck by those words, and it brought to his mind Revelation 7:17. This verse speaks of heaven and its fountains of living water and of the Lamb of God gathering there with His redeemed saints. This inspired Bliss to pen these words:

Will you meet me at the fountain, when I reach the glory land?
Will you meet me at the fountain, shall I clasp your friendly hand?
Other friends will give me welcome, other loving voices cheer;
There'll be music at the fountain; oh, be sure to meet me there!

Only those who are cleansed by Jesus' blood can hope to enjoy the fellowship and blessing found at those springs of living water. The question posed by Philip Bliss in that gospel song is one we all must answer. Will you meet me there?

—Henry Bosch

Philip Bliss became connected with D. L. Moody after the musician attended a Moody revival, noticed that the singing was not very good, and offered his services. He worked with Moody for a time, but when Moody asked him to help him with meetings in England, Bliss declined. Ira Sankey went instead.

BIRD SONG

Read: Psalm 104:24-35

Burst into jubilant song with music. —PSALM 98:4

Why do birds sing? Birds sing "because they can and because they must," says David Rothenberg, a professor at the New Jersey Institute of Technology. "Songs are used to attract mates and defend territories, but the form is much more than function. Nature is full of beauty, and of music."

Birds sing because they have a syrinx instead of a larynx. The syrinx is the bird's voice box, an organ that lies deep in a bird's chest and is uniquely fashioned for song. That, at least, is the natural explanation for their gift.

But I ask again, why do birds sing? Because their Creator put a song in their hearts. Each bird is "heaven's high and holy muse," said John Donne, created to draw our hearts up to our Creator. They are reminders that He has given us a song that we may sing His praise.

So when you hear God's little hymn-birds singing their hearts out, remember to sing your own song of salvation. Lift up your voice—harmonious, hoarse, or harsh—and join with them in praise to our Creator, Redeemer, and Lord.

The birds of the air "sing among the branches," Israel's poet observes. "[Therefore] I will sing to the LORD all my life; I will sing praise to my God as long as I live" (Psalm 104:12, 33).

—*David Roper*

———

John Donne (1572-1631), who lived most of his life in England and who was educated at Oxford University, penned such famous lines as "never send to know for whom the bell tolls; it tolls for thee," "no man is an island," and "death be not proud" in his many poems, sermons, and devotional works.

SCRIPTURAL SONGS

Read: Colossians 3:15-17

Let the message of Christ dwell among you richly . . . through psalms, hymns, and songs from the Spirit, singing to God with gratitude in your hearts. —COLOSSIANS 3:16

The beloved songwriter John W. Peterson was a master at using Scripture in his songs. When I was a teenager in the church choir, we performed his cantata *Jesus Is Coming* and sang these words taken from 2 Timothy 3:1–2: "In the last days perilous times shall come: for men shall be lovers of themselves." Then he wrote of the grim signs that we would recognize in the last days (vv. 2–7). The steady cadence of his music helps me remember that list even today.

While some of us have trouble memorizing verses from God's Word, something in our brain helps us to remember words in songs. If we analyze some of our favorite Christian songs and choruses, we find that they have been derived from Scripture. Thus, we can use the memory boost of music to hide away God-breathed words in our hearts (2 Timothy 3:16). Songs such as "Open the Eyes of My Heart" (Isaiah 6:9–10; Ephesians 1:18) or favorites like "Thy Word Have I Hid in My Heart" (Psalm 119:11, 105) are taken from the Bible. With these words hidden in our memory, a song of praise comes quickly to our lips.

No matter what kind of voice you have, when you sing the words of Scripture back to God, it is sweet music to His ears.

—*Cindy Hess Kasper*

Songwriter Paul Baloche didn't "write" the song "Open the Eyes of My Heart" as much as he "sang" it. As he was leading singing one day at his church and thinking of Ephesians 1:18, he simply began strumming his guitar and singing, "Open the eyes of my heart, Lord." On his blog he said that the song "pretty much rolled off my tongue."

※

THE MUSIC OF JOY

Read: Nehemiah 12:27-43

God had given them great joy. . . . The sound of rejoicing in Jerusalem could be heard far away. —NEHEMIAH 12:43

Several years ago, during a Christian men's conference in Boulder, Colorado, I stood with 50,000 men as we sang "All Hail the Power of Jesus' Name." The volume of the singing was incredible in the football stadium, and I've often wondered how it sounded outside. Could people hear it as they walked through a nearby park, sat on their patios, or drove by in cars? What impression did it leave with them?

That great sound of praise reminded me of what is described in today's Bible reading. The book of Nehemiah begins with a confession, continues with a construction project, and ends with a concert. The entire story is a study in God's faithfulness and power.

After years of hard work despite opposition, the wall of Jerusalem was rebuilt. At the dedication, two "thanksgiving choirs" stood on the wall to praise God. We are told that "God had given them great joy. . . . The sound of rejoicing in Jerusalem could be heard far away" (Nehemiah 12:42–43).

Joy cannot be contained. It must break out in praise to God through songs of thanksgiving. Whether those who hear our outpouring of joy understand it or not, it will resound as a chorus that cannot be ignored—the music of lives lived out in praise to God.

—David McCasland

The song "All Hail the Power of Jesus' Name" was first released to the public in 1779 in a magazine that was edited by Augustus Toplady, the man who wrote "Rock of Ages." The author of "All Hail . . . " was Edward Perronet (1726-1792), a friend of John and Charles Wesley.

HIS WAY

Read: Matthew 26:36-46

My Father, if it is possible, may this cup be taken from me. Yet not as I will, but as you will. —MATTHEW 26:39

A question about the title of a hymn took me back to a wonderful old song I grew up singing in church called "Let Him Have His Way with Thee." The chorus says:

> *His power can make you what you ought to be,*
> *His blood can cleanse your heart and make you free,*
> *His love can fill your soul, and you will see*
> *'Twas best for Him to have His way with thee.*

Even when we know that God's way is best for us, we may still struggle to obey Him. When Christ our Savior faced the horrible reality of bearing our sins on the cross, He agonized in prayer, saying, "My Father, if it is possible, may this cup be taken from me. Yet not as I will, but as you will" (Matthew 26:39). Jesus, who lived to do His Father's will, struggled and prayed, then willingly obeyed. And He can help us as we grapple with the difficult choices in our lives.

C. S. Lewis wrote: "There are only two kinds of people in the end: those who say to God, 'Thy will be done,' and those to whom God says, in the end, 'Thy will be done.' " If we continually choose our own way, He will eventually allow us to suffer the consequences.

It's best to surrender to God now. If we do, we'll have the assurance that His way is best for us.

—*David McCasland*

The man who wrote "Let Him Have His Way with Thee," Cyrus Nusbaum (1861–1937), was an ordained pastor. During World War I, he was a US Army captain who served in France.

"YES, WE'LL GATHER AT THE RIVER"

Read: Revelation 22:1-5

The angel showed me the river of the water of life, as clear as crystal,
flowing from the throne of God and of the Lamb.
—REVELATION 22:1

Many heart-stirring songs have been written by gifted Christian poets and composers who were inspired by real-life experiences. Pastor Robert Lowry (1826–1899), for example, penned the words and music of a hymn during an epidemic that was raging in the city of Philadelphia.

On a sultry afternoon in July, he sat in his study thinking about the many friends and loved ones who had recently been claimed by death. As he pondered the situation, he asked himself: *Why do hymn writers say so much about the mournful river of death we must cross but so little about the delightful river of life that Christians will enjoy in the new heaven and earth?* Moved by that thought, he wrote the verses that were to immortalize his name long after his excellent sermons were forgotten.

"Shall We Gather at the River?" remains a favorite today, more than 150 years after it was written. The first verse asks, "Shall we gather at the river, where bright angel feet have trod, with its crystal tide forever flowing by the throne of God?"

The assuring answer is given in the chorus, "Yes, we'll gather at the river, the beautiful, the beautiful river, gather with the saints at the river that flows by the throne of God."

Friend, when eternity dawns, will you be a member of the joyous company of the redeemed who will gather to praise the Lord at that crystal stream?

—*Henry Bosch*

This song was sung at the memorial service of US Supreme Court Justice William O. Douglas in 1980.

NOW IS THE TIME

Read: Luke 2:8-20

Glory to God in the highest heaven. —LUKE 2:14

During our church's Christmas celebration, I watched the choir members assemble in front of the congregation while the music director rifled through papers on a slim black stand. The instruments began, and the singers launched into the well-known song "Come, Now Is the Time to Worship."

Although I expected to hear a time-honored Christmas carol, I smiled at the appropriate choice of music. Earlier that week I had been reading Luke's account of Jesus' birth, and I noticed that the first Christmas lacked our modern-day parties, gifts, and feasting—but it did include worship.

After the angel announced Jesus' birth to some wide-eyed shepherds, a chorus of angels began "praising God and saying, 'Glory to God in the highest heaven' " (Luke 2:13–14). The shepherds responded by running to Bethlehem where they found the newborn King lying in a barnyard bassinet. They returned to their fields "glorifying and praising God for all the things they had heard and seen" (v. 20). Coming face to face with the Son inspired the shepherds to worship the Father.

Today, consider your response to Jesus' arrival on earth. Is there room for worship in your heart to celebrate His birth?

—*Jennifer Benson Schuldt*

According to his own telling of the creation of "Come, Now Is the Time to Worship," Brian Doerksen wrote it while living in London. One day during a wilderness time in his life, he took an early morning walk. As he strolled through his neighborhood, the idea and the melody began to come to him. He sang this first part of the song over and over until he arrived at home and could put the music and words down on paper. He worked on the song for about a week before introducing it to his church, where he was a worship leader.

ONLY FROM ABOVE

Read: Psalm 104:21-28

Every good and perfect gift is from above, coming down from the Father of the heavenly lights, who does not change like shifting shadows.
—JAMES 1:17

The sustaining and providing hand of our loving heavenly Father is always outstretched toward us. Yet we are often prone to forget the source of all the good that comes into our lives.

In 1808, just a year before the death of Franz Joseph Haydn, a grand performance of his outstanding oratorio *The Creation* took place in Vienna. The composer himself was there for the occasion. Old and feeble, he was brought into the great hall in a wheelchair. His presence caused an electrifying enthusiasm in the audience. As the orchestra and chorus burst forth with full power into the passage, "And there was light," a crescendo of applause broke out. Moved by this response, the elderly musician struggled to his feet. Summoning all his strength, he raised his trembling arms upward, crying, "No, no! Not from me, but from thence—from heaven above comes all!" Although he fell back exhausted in his chair and had to be carried from the hall, the old master had made his point in a dramatic and unforgettable manner.

Man constantly needs to be reminded that all his blessings are derived from the Creator. The Bible says, "He causes his sun to rise on the evil and the good, and sends rain on the righteous and the unrighteous" (Matthew 5:45). The bountiful provisions for our physical needs and the amazing grace that makes us joint heirs with Christ all come from God. Let us acknowledge our dependence upon Him and humbly say, "When I consider your heavens, the work of your fingers, the moon and the stars, which you have set in place, what is mankind that you are mindful of them?" (Psalm 8:3–4). Surely "every good and perfect gift is from above."

—*Paul Van Gorder*

According to biographer Dave Massey, Franz Joseph Haydn (1732–1809) was so taken with doing justice to the creation in the work of the same name that, in Haydn's words, "Every day I fell to my knees and prayed to God to grant me the strength" to finish it. He was sixty-six years old when he finished the oratorio.

PUBLIC PRAISE

Read: Psalm 96

Declare his glory among the nations, his marvelous deeds among all peoples. —PSALM 96:3

I love the YouTube video of people in a food court of a mall, who in the midst of their ordinary lives were suddenly interrupted by someone who stood up and boldly began singing the "Hallelujah Chorus." To the surprise of everyone, another person got up and joined the chorus, and then another, and another. Soon the food court was resounding with the celebrative harmonies of Handel's masterpiece. A local opera company had planted their singers in strategic places so that they could joyfully interject the glory of God into the everyday lives of lunching shoppers.

Every time I watch that video, it moves me to tears. It reminds me that bringing the glory of God into the ordinary situations of our world through the beautiful harmonies of Christlikeness is exactly what we are called to do. Think of intentionally interjecting God's grace into a situation where some undeserving soul needs a second chance; of sharing the love of Christ with someone who is needy; of being the hands of Jesus that lift up a weary friend; or of bringing peace to a confusing and chaotic situation.

As the psalmist reminds us, we have the high and holy privilege of declaring "his glory among the nations, his marvelous deeds among all peoples" (Psalm 96:3).

—*Joe Stowell*

As the food court rendition moved along, patrons began to join in, to stand, to take photos with their phones—and when the song was over, they erupted in applause. Many were in tears as God's praise rang throughout that section of the mall.

HAPPINESS AND FAITH

Read: Romans 8:28-39

May the God of hope fill you with all joy and peace as you trust in him, so that you may overflow with hope by the power of the Holy Spirit.
—ROMANS 15:13

The chorus of the old hymn "At the Cross" concludes with these cheerful words: "And now I am happy all the day!" I don't know about you, but I can't honestly say that just because I know Jesus as my Savior I'm happy all day. I'm a rather optimistic person and I don't let much get me down, but some circumstances don't warm my heart and make me smile.

Troubles may make us wonder: Isn't our faith supposed to make us happy all the time? Shouldn't Jesus shelter us from harm and danger?

Some people teach these things, but the Bible doesn't. God's Word makes it clear that we will have trouble. In Romans 8, for example, the apostle Paul talked frankly about tough times we could face (vv. 35–39). The fact is, Jesus doesn't protect us from all trouble, but His love and His companionship guide us as we go through it.

A more realistic attitude than being "happy all the day" is one stated by a Christian who said, "Now that I'm saved, I'm happier when I am down than I was when I was happy before I was saved."

With Jesus Christ, we can have real joy and make it through even the bad times.

—*Dave Branon*

———

Fanny Crosby, who penned so many of the timeless classics in our hymnbooks, was greatly influenced by the song "At the Cross," which was penned by Isaac Watts. Apparently she was attending revival meetings at a crisis time in her life, and the words "Here, Lord, I give my self away 'tis all that I can do" enlightened her soul.

ALL IS WELL

Read: Psalm 46:1-3

Keep your lives from the love of money and be content with what you have, because God has said, "Never will I leave you; never will I forsake you."
–HEBREWS 13:5

Recently, my husband and I were reacquainted with a young man we had known as a child many years ago. We fondly reminisced about a Christmas program when Matthew had sung—in a perfect boy soprano—the song "All Is Well" by Wayne Kirkpatrick and Michael W. Smith. It was a wonderful memory of a song beautifully sung. It is a song that speaks of the birth of Emmanuel—our Savior and our Lord, and it reminds us of those glorious words in the song's title.

To hear the words "all is well" at Christmastime is comforting to many. But some people are unable to absorb the message because their lives are in turmoil. They've experienced the loss of a loved one, persistent unemployment, a serious illness, or depression that will not go away. Their hearts loudly cry out, "All is not well—not for me!"

But for those of us who celebrate the birth of our Savior— despite the dark night of the soul we may experience—all is well because of Christ. We are not alone in our pain. God is beside us and promises never to leave (Hebrews 13:5). He promises to supply all our needs (Philippians 4:19). And He promises us the amazing gift of eternal life (John 10:27–28).

As we review God's promises, we can agree with the poet John Greenleaf Whittier, who wrote, "Before me, even as behind, God is, and all is well."

—Cindy Hess Kasper

Michael W. Smith wrote the music for the song "All Is Well" before he had the words. Later he asked a few people, including Amy Grant and his wife, Debbie, to pen the lyrics. Grammy Award-winning composer Wayne Kirkpatrick finally came up with the words.

CHANGE OF PLANS

Read: Proverbs 16:1-9

In their hearts humans plan their course, but the Lord *establishes their steps.* —PROVERBS 16:9

It was Christmas Eve in Oberndorf, Austria, in 1818. Joseph Mohr, the vicar of the church, had written a new song for the Christmas Eve service and the organist Franz Gruber had set it to music. But the organ in the village church broke down. So Gruber grabbed a guitar and accompanied Mohr in the first-ever rendition of "Silent Night."

The story doesn't end there, however. When a man came to fix the organ, Gruber tested it by playing the new song. The repairman liked the song so much that he took a copy of it back to his own village. There, four daughters of a village glove-maker learned the song and began singing it in concerts all over the region. Because of that faulty organ, this new Christmas song blessed people all over Austria—and eventually the world.

When things break or when plans change, how should we respond? Often we fret and worry because we don't have the control we would like to have. That's when we need to step back, trust God, and wait to see how He will use the situation for His glory. The changes in our lives may not give the world something as remarkable as "Silent Night," but because God is in charge we can be sure that "all is calm, all is bright."

—*Dave Branon*

Only one other song written by Joseph Mohr (1792-1848) and Franz Gruber has been discovered. It is called "Te Deum," and it was not found until 2006 among the archives of a parish where Mohr once served.

MORE THAN A CONQUEROR

Read: 2 Corinthians 12:1-10

We are more than conquerors through him who loved us.
—ROMANS 8:37

Fanny Crosby, composer of thousands of songs, was truly "more than a conqueror." When she was only six weeks old, faulty treatment of an eye infection resulted in lifelong blindness. By age eight, having fought and won over discouragement, she wrote this poem:

Oh, what a happy soul am I, although I cannot see!
I am resolved that in this world contented I shall be.
How many blessings I enjoy that other people don't.
To weep and sigh because I'm blind, I cannot—and I won't!

Instead of weeping and sighing, Fanny Crosby dedicated her blindness to God. Out of her rich Christian experience she composed numerous gospel hymns. In her testimonial song "Blessed Assurance," she seemed to forget that she was blind. Phrases like "Visions of rapture now burst on my sight" or "Watching and waiting, looking above" expressed what she called "a foretaste of glory divine."

Do you long to know and apply her secret? Consider this: While many of us seek Christ for what we can get, Fanny Crosby sought Christ for what she could become through Him—more than a conqueror (Romans 8:37). Even through times of extreme distress, God's grace is sufficient (2 Corinthians 12:9), and He is lovingly working to make us more like His Son.

We all need to ask ourselves: Is our Christian life about getting or becoming?

—*Joanie Yoder*

Consider this background: Mistreated by a charlatan posing as a doctor, Fanny Crosby became blind at two months. Shortly after that, her father died. Struggling to survive, her mother became a maid. A grandmother was forced to raise her. That sounds like a recipe for a failed life, but not for Fanny Crosby. Her faith and her determination enabled her to write this poem at age eight and to address the Congress of the United States at age twenty-three.

))((

THE DOCTOR'S BIBLE

Read: Acts 26:9-18

*Therefore, if anyone is in Christ, the new creation has come:
The old has gone, the new is here!* —2 CORINTHIANS 5:17

William Mackay (1839–1885) had been brought up by a godly, praying mother who gave him a Bible with his name inscribed inside the front cover when he went off to medical school. During his training, he renounced his mother's faith and began to drink heavily. He even pawned his Bible so he could buy more liquor.

He continued with his education and indeed became a medical doctor. One day as he tended an accident victim, the injured person asked Dr. Mackay if he would send for the man's landlady. He wanted her to bring "the book."

The patient never recovered, and after he died, Dr. Mackay was curious about what book the man requested. A nurse told him where to look, and he found the book—a Bible.

The doctor opened the Bible and when he did he saw his name written inside. This was the same book he had pawned years earlier to fuel his thirst for alcohol. Remembering his mother's love and under deep conviction of sin, Mackay went to his room and began praying for God's mercy. Recalling John 3:16, he prayed for forgiveness and trusted Jesus as His Savior.

Not long afterward, he penned the lyrics of the gospel song "Revive Us Again." The opening words were part of his new witness for Christ: "We praise Thee, O God, for the Son of Thy love, for Jesus who died and is now gone above."

Friend, the Lord Jesus can transform you as He did William Mackay and use you for His glory.

—Henry Bosch

Once in Australia two large groups of people, separated by two city blocks, sang parts of "Revive Us Again" antiphonally. One group of 80,000 sang "Hallelujah," and the other group of a similar size sang "Thine the glory."

SCRIPTURE INDEX
OF KEY VERSES

OUR DAILY BREAD WRITERS

HENRY BOSCH

The first editor of *Our Daily Bread,* Henry loved to sing—and actually did some recording for Radio Bible Class in its early years.

DAVE BRANON

An editor with Discovery House, Dave has been involved with *Our Daily Bread* since the 1980s. He has written several books, including *Beyond the Valley* and *Stand Firm,* both Discovery House publications.

ANNE CETAS

After becoming a Christian in her late teens, Anne was introduced to *Our Daily Bread* right away and began reading it. Now she reads it for a living as the senior content editor of *Our Daily Bread.*

BILL CROWDER

A former pastor who is now an associate teacher for Our Daily Bread Ministries, Bill travels extensively as a Bible conference teacher, sharing God's truths with fellow believers in Malaysia and Singapore and other places where the ministry has international offices.

DENNIS DEHAAN

When Henry Bosch retired, Dennis became the second managing editor of *Our Daily Bread.* A former pastor, he loved preaching and teaching the Word of God.

RICHARD DEHAAN

Son of the founder of Our Daily Bread Ministries, Dr. M. R. DeHaan, Richard was responsible for the ministry's entrance into television. Under his leadership, *Day of Discovery*, the ministry's long-running TV program, made its debut in 1968.

DAVID EGNER

A retired Our Daily Bread Ministries editor and longtime *Our Daily Bread* writer, David was also a college professor during his working career. In fact, he was a writing instructor for both Anne Cetas and Julie Ackerman Link at Cornerstone University.

DENNIS FISHER

As a research editor at Our Daily Bread Ministries, Dennis uses his theological training to guarantee biblical accuracy. He is also an expert in C. S. Lewis studies.

VERNON GROUNDS

A longtime college president (Denver Seminary) and board member for Our Daily Bread Ministries, Vernon's life story was told in the Discovery House book *Transformed by Love*.

CINDY HESS KASPER

An editor for the Our Daily Bread Ministries publication *Our Daily Journey*, Cindy began writing for *Our Daily Bread* in 2006.

JULIE ACKERMAN LINK

A book editor by profession, Julie wrote for *Our Daily Bread* from 2000 to 2015. Her book *Above All, Love* was published in

2008 by Discovery House. Julie passed away on April 10, 2015, after a lengthy battle with cancer.

DAVID MCCASLAND

Living in Colorado, David enjoys the beauty of God's grandeur as displayed in the Rocky Mountains. An accomplished biographer, David has written several books, including *Oswald Chambers: Abandoned to God* and *Eric Liddell: Pure Gold.*

HADDON ROBINSON

Haddon has taught hundreds of young preachers the art of preaching. He is former president of Denver Seminary and served for many years as a professor at Gordon-Conwell Theological Seminary.

DAVID ROPER

David Roper lives in Idaho, where he takes advantage of the natural beauty of his state. He has been writing for *Our Daily Bread* since 2000, and he has published several successful books with Discovery House.

JENNIFER BENSON SCHULDT

Chicagoan Jennifer Schuldt writes from the perspective of a mom of a growing family. She has written for *Our Daily Bread* since 2010, and she also pens articles for another Our Daily Bread Ministries publication: *Our Daily Journey.*

JOE STOWELL

As president of Cornerstone University, Joe stays connected to today's young adults in a leadership role. A popular speaker and a former pastor, Joe has written a number of books over the years, including *Strength for the Journey* and *Jesus Nation*.

HERB VANDER LUGT

For many years, Herb was the research editor at Our Daily Bread Ministries, responsible for checking the biblical accuracy of the booklets published by the ministry. A World War II veteran, Herb spent several years as a pastor before his Our Daily Bread Ministries tenure began.

PAUL VAN GORDER

A writer for *Our Daily Bread* in the 1980s and 1990s, Paul was a noted pastor and Bible teacher—both in the Atlanta area where he lived and through the *Day of Discovery* TV program.

JOANIE YODER

Joanie and her husband established a Christian rehabilitation center for drug addicts in England many years ago. Widowed in 1982, she wrote with hope about true dependence on God and His life-changing power. Joanie was the author of the book *Finding the God-Dependent Life*.